D(
W
dr(
hu

one day become a household word. Introduced in 1950, the Original Bundt® Pan, with its unique fluted design and signature hole in the center, was inspired by a well-used ring cake mold brought to us by two immigrant women in our Minneapolis, Minnesota community. Though not an instant success by any means, the Bundt pan gained recognition over the next couple decades, and in the early 1970's we published the first edition of this recipe book. Back then we were amazed and grateful that several million people had purchased one of our Bundt pans.

Many years have passed, and our pans have stood the test of time. Today, over 73 million Nordic Ware Bundt pans are in use. Pans and recipes are passed lovingly from one generation to the next. Beauty shots of cakes and recipes (from "the wacky to the divine" to quote a recent newspaper article), are featured in print and online daily-- and Bundt cakes are an iconic centerpiece at gatherings of all kinds. New designs and sizes continue to be added to the delight of bakers and collectors worldwide.

Customers asked us to update our original recipe book, and this is the result. The many vintage recipes included were gathered long ago from friends, professional and personal, or developed in my own kitchen. We have added a few new ones too! Times and eating habits have changed, but everyone appreciates a lovely, delicious dessert—and few desserts can consistently produce the "wow" effect of a Bundt cake. Whether you inherited your Bundt pan, received it as a gift, or bought it for yourself, we hope you will enjoy these heritage recipes, both savory and sweet, from our company's early days.

Happy baking!

Dotty Dalquist

Dorothy Dalquist

BAKING THE *perfect* BUNDT® CAKE

1. Prepare the pan

- Using a pastry brush, lightly coat the entire inside surface of the pan with solid vegetable shortening or softened butter.

- Dust lightly with flour. We recommend a cake flour such as Wondra® for best results. (Cake flour has a lower protein content than all-purpose flour, making it less "sticky"). For chocolate cakes, "flouring" the pan with cocoa powder eliminates any white film on the exterior of the cake.

- Briskly tap pan several times with your hands to distribute the flour evenly, then turn the pan upside down over sink to remove excess flour.

- If you prefer spray, we recommend using a nonstick baking spray containing flour, such as Baker's Joy® or Pam® Baking. Apply just before putting the batter in the pan, and spray the inside thoroughly but not too heavily, holding the can 8″ to 10″ from the pan. It's important to use a pastry brush to smooth the spray evenly into each groove so the pan's interior is consistently coated. Briefly turn the pan upside down on a paper towel, allowing excess oil to drain. Avoid using regular cooking spray as it causes a gummy residue to build up on the nonstick surface of the pan, making it more likely that future cakes will stick.

2. Avoid bubbles in the batter

- Slowly pour batter into one corner of the pan and allow the batter to gradually fill the pan from that position rather than circling the pan with the bowl of batter.

- Fill ⅔ to ¾ full to allow room for the cake to rise.

- Tap the filled cake pan on a cutting board or counter a few times to dissipate air pockets and to help the batter settle into the details of the pan.

3. Bake and cool

- Place pan on the center rack of preheated oven.

- Bake for time indicated. The best test for cake doneness is inserting a cake tester or toothpick into the center of the cake. If it comes out clean, the cake is done.

- Remove pan from oven using hot pads on each side.

- For most recipes, cool 10–15 minutes in pan before inverting. For pans with miniature molds, cooling for 5 minutes should be enough.

- With hot pads, gently shake the pan from side to side to loosen the cake from the pan. You should hear and feel the cake shifting slightly in the pan. A plastic spatula may be used to carefully loosen the cake around the center tube and sides if sticking persists.
- Note: pans with dark interior coatings will bake faster than light colored pans; simply reduce the oven temperature by 25 degrees to accommodate darker coatings.

4. Invert, cool and decorate
- Invert cake onto serving plate or cooling rack; continue to cool as recipe directs.
- Dust with powdered sugar or drizzle with your favorite glaze when completely cool.

ADJUSTING RECIPES TO FIT VARIOUS NORDIC WARE BUNDT® PANS

Most recipes may be adapted to fit the various pans in our line using the guidelines below. Times may vary with different ovens and altitudes.

Some recipes require a shorter or longer baking time and ovens will vary. When adjusting recipes for different size Bundt pans, always start testing for doneness a few minutes before the lowest baking time recommended. If pan is ¾ full and there is batter remaining, use it to bake a muffin or two rather than overfilling the Bundt pan.

9- to 12-cup Bundt Pan
45–60 minutes

1-cup muffin pan
18–22 minutes

5- to 6-cup Bundt Pan
25–30 minutes

½-cup muffin pan
12–17 minutes

3-cup Bundt Pan
20–25 minutes

HELPFUL HINTS FOR CLEANING NORDIC WARE BUNDT® PANS

We recommend hand washing for all Nordic Ware baking pans. They may be soaked in hot soapy water and washed with a textured scrubber or a brush that is safe for nonstick coatings. For any residue remaining in small crevices, use a small brush, toothpick or the popular Ultimate Bundt® Cleaning Tool. Avoid automatic dishwashers as the detergent is caustic and can damage the pan's nonstick coating.

TABLE OF CONTENTS

Copyright © 2019 by Nordic Ware®
5005 County Road 25, Minneapolis, MN 55416

Nordic Ware®, Bundt® Pan and Bundtlette® are registered trademarks of Northland Aluminum Products, Inc.

Designed by Mindy Gallagher
Recipe Editing by LoAnn Mockler

For assistance or questions, please call
Nordic Ware Consumer Service at 1-877-466-7342 (toll-free).

ISBN 978-0-578-60593-7

www.nordicware.com

Cakes
FROM SCRATCH

Cakes from scratch

NOEL FRUITCAKE

½ cup	raisins
½ cup	diced, candied fruit
2 tbsp	brandy
½ cup	shortening
1 cup	sugar
1	egg, slightly beaten
1 cup	chopped walnuts
2 cups	all-purpose flour
1 tsp	baking soda
1 tsp	cinnamon
½ tsp	salt
½ tsp	nutmeg
¼ tsp	ground cloves
¼ tsp	allspice
1 cup	applesauce

Preheat oven to 350°F. Grease and flour a 10- or 12-cup Bundt Pan.

In small bowl, soak raisins and fruit in brandy. In large bowl, cream shortening and sugar until light and fluffy. Add egg, raisins, fruit and nuts; mix well. In medium bowl, whisk together dry ingredients. Add alternately with applesauce to creamed mixture, mixing well after each addition. Pour batter into prepared pan.

Bake for 50 minutes or until cake tests done.

Cool in pan 10 minutes; invert on wire rack or serving plate to complete cooling. Wrap tightly in foil to store. Store in cool place.

Just before serving, drizzle melted apple or currant jelly over top, if desired.

CHEESY CHERRY CAKE

8 oz	cream cheese, softened
1 cup	butter, softened
1½ cups	sugar
1½ tsp	vanilla
4	eggs
2¼ cups	all-purpose flour, divided
1½ tsp	baking powder
¾ cup	well-drained,chopped maraschino cherries
½ cup	chopped pecans
½ cup	finely chopped pecans

Preheat oven to 350°F.

In large bowl, thoroughly blend softened cream cheese, butter, sugar and vanilla. Add eggs, one at a time, mixing well after each addition. In medium bowl, whisk together 2 cups of flour with the baking powder and gradually add to creamed mixture. Combine remaining flour with cherries and ½ cup chopped pecans; fold into batter.

Grease a 10- or 12-cup Bundt Pan and sprinkle with ½ cup finely chopped pecans. Pour batter into prepared pan and bake for 60–65 minutes or until cake tests done.

Cool in pan 10–15 minutes; invert on wire rack or serving plate to complete cooling. Top with Basic Vanilla Glaze. Garnish with cherries and pecans.

HOLIDAY ALMOND TEA CAKE

1⅓ cups	butter
4 tbsp	frozen orange juice concentrate, thawed
1	grated orange peel
¾ tsp	vanilla
½ tsp	salt
5	whole eggs, at room temperature
5	egg yolks, at room temperature
1⅓ cups	sugar
2 cups	all-purpose flour
⅓ cup	cornstarch
1 tsp	baking powder
24	whole blanched almonds

Preheat oven to 350°F.

Combine butter, orange juice concentrate, orange peel, vanilla and salt in saucepan; stir over low heat until butter is melted. Let cool to lukewarm.

Beat eggs, egg yolks and sugar in large bowl until triple in volume. In medium bowl, whisk together flour, cornstarch and baking powder; sprinkle over egg mixture and fold together. By hand, gently fold in orange-butter mixture until there is no trace of butter.

Grease a 10- or 12-cup Bundt Pan and arrange almonds in bottom of pan in flutes, securing nuts with a dab of butter. Pour batter into prepared pan. Bake for 50 minutes or until cake tests done.

Cool in pan 10–15 minutes; invert on wire rack or serving plate to complete cooling.

PEANUT BRITTLE CRUNCH CAKE

⅔ cup	butter
1⅓ cups	firmly packed brown sugar
⅔ cup	sugar
2⅔ cups	all-purpose flour
1⅓ cups	buttermilk
1½ tsp	baking soda
2	eggs
½ tsp	salt
1½ tsp	vanilla
1 cup	crushed peanut brittle
⅓ cup	chopped nuts

Preheat oven to 350°F. Grease and flour a 10- or 12-cup Bundt Pan.

In large bowl, combine sugars and flour; cut in butter until crumbly. Set aside ½ cup to be used in filling. To remainder add buttermilk, baking soda, eggs, salt and vanilla; beat well. Pour ½ of batter into prepared pan. Combine reserved sugar-flour mixture with peanut brittle and nuts. Pour evenly over batter in pan. Add remaining batter.

Bake for 50–60 minutes or until cake tests done. Cool in pan 10–15 minutes; invert on wire rack or serving plate to complete cooling. Sprinkle with confectioners' sugar.

Variation: Toffee bars may be substituted for peanut brittle. Use approximately 4–5¾ oz bars. It is easier to crush toffee if it is first frozen.

COFFEE POUND CAKE

5 tbsp	instant coffee granules
½ cup	hot milk
1⅓ cups	butter, softened
1½ cups	sugar
4	eggs
2⅔ cups	all-purpose flour
3 tsp	baking powder
½ tsp	salt
1 cup	chopped walnuts

Preheat oven to 350°F. Grease and flour a 10- or 12-cup Bundt Pan.

Dissolve coffee in milk; let cool. In large bowl, cream butter with sugar; add eggs, one at a time, and beat well after each addition.

In medium bowl, whisk together flour, baking powder and salt; add alternately with milk-coffee mixture to creamed mixture. Fold in nuts. Pour into prepared pan.

Bake for 50–60 minutes or until cake tests done. Cool in pan 10–15 minutes; invert on wire rack or serving plate to complete cooling.

Top with Vanilla or Coffee Glaze.

SWEDISH RUM CAKE

4	eggs
1¾ cups	sugar
3 tsp	rum extract
1 tsp	grated lemon peel
2½ cups	all-purpose flour
1¾ tsp	baking powder
⅔ cup	milk
⅔ cup	butter, melted

Glaze:

⅓ cup	sugar
⅓ cup	water
⅓ cup	rum

Preheat oven to 350°F. Grease and flour the Pound Cake/Angel Food Cake Pan.

In a large bowl, beat eggs, sugar, rum extract and lemon peel until light and fluffy. In a medium bowl, whisk together flour and baking powder; add to creamed mixture alternately with milk. Stir in butter. Pour into prepared pan.

Bake for 50–60 minutes or until cake tests done. Cool in pan 10–15 minutes; invert on wire rack or serving plate.

In saucepan, combine sugar and water for glaze and cook until sugar is dissolved. Cool and add rum. Pour glaze over cake. May serve warm or cold.

OLD DOMINION POUND CAKE

2¼ cups	all-purpose flour
1¼ cups	sugar
¼ tsp	baking soda
1½ cups	butter, softened
2 tbsp	lemon juice
2¼ tsp	vanilla
8	large eggs, separated
⅛ tsp	salt
1 cup	sugar
1½ tsp	cream of tartar

Preheat oven to 325°F. Grease and flour the Pound Cake/Angel Food Cake Pan.

In large bowl, blend flour, 1¼ cups sugar and baking soda. Blend butter into flour mixture; add lemon juice and vanilla. At low speed, beat in egg yolks, one at a time, until blended.

In separate bowl, beat egg whites until frothy; add salt, then gradually add 1 cup sugar with cream of tartar, beating well after each addition. Beat until soft peaks form. Gently fold beaten egg whites into cake batter.

Pour batter into prepared pan. Using a rubber spatula or knife, gently cut through cake batter one or two times.

Bake for 1½ hours or until cake tests done. (Do not peak at cake during the first hour of baking.) Turn off oven and let cake remain in oven 15 minutes. Remove to cool in pan 15 minutes then invert on wire rack or serving plate to complete cooling. Sprinkle with confectioners' sugar.

GEORGIAN CHOCOLATE POUND CAKE

1 cup	butter, softened
3 cups	sugar
3 cups	all-purpose flour
1 cup	unsweetened cocoa
3 tsp	baking powder
1 tsp	salt
1½ cups	milk
3	eggs
¼ cup	evaporated milk
1 tbsp	vanilla

Preheat oven to 325°F. Grease and flour a 10- or 12-cup Bundt Pan.

In large bowl, cream butter and sugar until light and fluffy. Whisk together flour, cocoa, baking powder and salt. Add dry ingredients alternately with milk to butter mixture. Beat 3 minutes. Add eggs, one at a time, beating after each addition. Add evaporated milk and vanilla; beat 2 minutes. Pour batter into prepared pan.

Bake for 1½ hours or until cake tests done. Cool in pan 10–15 minutes; invert on wire rack or serving plate to complete cooling. Sprinkle with confectioners' sugar.

NUTTY ORANGE CAKE

1½ cups	butter, divided, softened
1½ cups	sugar, divided
½ cup	finely crushed bread crumbs
1 ½ cups	finely chopped nuts
1 tbsp	grated orange peel
1 tsp	vanilla
4	eggs
½ cup	orange marmalade
3 cups	all-purpose flour
1 tsp	salt
1 tsp	baking soda
1 tsp	baking powder
½ cup	orange juice
½ cup	evaporated milk

Preheat oven to 350°F.

Combine in small bowl ½ cup each butter, sugar, finely crushed bread crumbs and finely chopped nuts (reserving leftovers of each for cake batter). Grease a 10- or 12-cup Bundt Pan. Press mixture into the sides and bottom of pan. Place pan in refrigerator and chill while making cake.

In large mixing bowl, combine remaining butter, sugar, orange peel and vanilla; cream thoroughly until light and fluffy. Add eggs, one at a time, and beat well after each addition. Blend in marmalade. In medium bowl, whisk together flour, salt, baking soda and baking powder. Add to creamed mixture alternately with combined orange juice and evaporated milk. Stir in remaining chopped nuts and blend.

Turn into prepared pan and bake for 55–60 minutes or until cake tests done. Cool in pan 10–15 minutes; invert on wire rack or serving plate to complete cooling.

JACKIE'S POUND CAKE

1 cup	butter, softened
3 cups	sugar
6	large eggs
3 cups	cake flour
½ pint	whipping cream
1 tsp	vanilla
½ tsp	lemon extract
½ tsp	almond extract

Grease and flour a 10- or 12-cup Bundt Pan.

In large bowl, cream butter and sugar until light and fluffy. Add eggs, one at a time. Add ½ of the flour and ½ of the cream. Mix well. Add remaining flour and cream. Add extracts.

Pour batter into prepared pan and put it in a cold oven. Set oven at 300°F and bake about 1¾ hours. Cool in pan 10–15 minutes; invert on wire rack or serving plate to complete cooling. Sprinkle with confectioners' sugar or top with Basic Vanilla Glaze and almonds.

CHOCOLATE RIBBON POUND CAKE

¾ cup	butter, softened
2 cups	sugar
1 tsp	vanilla
2	eggs
2 cups	all-purpose flour
1 tsp	baking powder
¼ tsp	salt
8 oz	sour cream

Filling:

6 oz	semi sweet chocolate chips
½ cup	chopped nuts
⅓ cup	sweetened condensed milk
1 tbsp	grated orange peel

Preheat oven to 350°F. Grease and flour a 10- or 12-cup Bundt Pan.

In small bowl, combine all filling ingredients; set aside. In large bowl, cream butter, sugar and vanilla until light and fluffy. Add eggs, one at a time, beating well after each addition. In medium bowl, whisk together flour, baking powder and salt. Add to creamed mixture with sour cream and blend until moistened; beat 3 minutes at medium speed.

Spoon ½ of batter into prepared pan; spoon filling in center of batter, not touching sides of pan. Spoon remaining batter into pan to cover filling.

Bake for 65–80 minutes or until cake tests done. Cool in pan 10–15 minutes; invert on wire rack or serving plate to complete cooling. Top with a thin orange glaze.

CHOCOLATE CHIP DATE CAKE

1 cup	finely cut dates
1 cup	boiling water
1 tsp	baking soda
1 cup	shortening
1 cup	sugar
2	eggs
1 tsp	vanilla
2 cups	all-purpose flour
2 tbsp	unsweetened cocoa
½ tsp	salt
6 oz	chocolate chips
½ cup	chopped nuts

Preheat oven to 350°F. Grease and flour a 10- or 12-cup Bundt Pan.

In medium bowl, pour boiling water over cut dates. Let cool; add baking soda. In large bowl, cream shortening; add sugar, eggs and vanilla and beat well; add cooled date mixture. In medium bowl, whisk together flour, cocoa and salt. Add flour mixture to creamed mixture; fold in chocolate chips and nuts. Pour batter into prepared pan.

Bake for 45 minutes or until cake tests done. Cool in pan 10–15 minutes; invert on wire rack or serving plate to complete cooling. Sprinkle with confectioners' sugar.

Cakes from scratch

GATHER ROUND POUND CAKE

6 oz	butterscotch morsels
2 tbsp	instant coffee granules
¼ cup	water
1 cup	butter, softened
1½ cups	sugar
3 cups	all-purpose flour
½ tsp	baking soda
¼ tsp	salt
½ tsp	baking powder
¾ cup	buttermilk
4	eggs

Preheat oven to 325°F. Grease and flour a 10- or 12-cup Bundt Pan.

Melt butterscotch morsels, instant coffee and water in a double boiler. In large bowl, cream butter and sugar. Blend in butterscotch mixture.

In medium bowl, whisk together flour, baking soda, salt and baking powder; add to creamed mixture alternately with buttermilk. Add eggs, one at a time, beating well after each addition. Pour batter into prepared pan.

Bake for 60–70 minutes or until cake tests done. Cool in pan 10–15 minutes; invert on wire rack or serving plate to complete cooling. Sprinkle with confectioners' sugar or top with Vanilla, Butterscotch or Coffee Glaze.

COCOA APPLE CAKE

3	eggs
2 cups	sugar
1 cup	butter, softened
2½ cups	all-purpose flour
2 tbsp	unsweetened cocoa
1 tsp	baking soda
1 tsp	cinnamon
1 tsp	allspice
½ cup	water
1 cup	finely chopped nuts
½ cup	chocolate chips
2	apples, cored and grated or finely chopped (2 cups)
2 tsp	vanilla

Preheat oven to 325°F. Grease and flour a 10- or 12-cup Bundt Pan.

In large bowl, beat eggs, sugar and butter until fluffy. In medium bowl, whisk together flour, cocoa, baking soda, cinnamon and allspice. Add to creamed mixture along with water and mix well. Fold in nuts, chocolate chips, apples and vanilla. Pour batter into prepared pan.

Bake for 60–70 minutes or until cake tests done. Cool in pan 10–15 minutes; invert on wire rack or serving plate to complete cooling. Sprinkle with confectioners' sugar or top with a Spice or Coffee Glaze.

CARDAMOM CREAM BUNDT CAKE

3 cups	all-purpose flour
1½ cup	baker's sugar (finely granulated)
3 tsp	baking powder
1 tbsp	cardamom, freshly and finely ground with mortar and pestle
¼ tsp	kosher salt
5	large eggs, room temperature
2¼ cups	heavy whipping cream, room temperature
1 tsp	vanilla extract

Glaze:

2 cups	confectioners' sugar, sifted
1 tbsp	butter
½ tsp	vanilla extract
1 tsp	finely ground cardamom
3 tbsp	whole milk or cream

Preheat oven to 350°F. Grease and flour a 10- or 12- cup Bundt pan, or use a baking spray that contains flour.

In the bowl of a mixer fitted with a flat beater, combine first five ingredients. Add eggs one at a time and blend until incorporated. Scrape down sides of bowl. Add cream in a slow, steady stream and vanilla. Beat mixture on medium high for 2 minutes.

Pour batter into prepared Bundt pan, no more than ¾ full to avoid overflow during baking. Find a firm surface such as a cutting board and firmly tap filled pan against the surface to remove air bubbles from the pan's crevices. This will result in a dense, bubble-free cake exterior. Bake 60 minutes or until a toothpick comes out clean. Cool in pan precisely 10 minutes before inverting on a cooling rack.

While cake is baking, prepare glaze mixture by combining ingredients in a small saucepan on the stove. Whisk to combine, and bring to a simmer, then remove from heat and allow to cool.

If you prefer a thinner glaze, apply to warm cake just after inverting from pan. If a thicker glaze is desired, allow cake and glaze to cool completely to room temperature, and pour glaze on just before serving. You can thicken or thin the consistency by adding additional confectioners' sugar or milk if necessary.

Cakes from scratch

TUNNEL OF FUDGE CAKE

1¾ cups	butter, softened
1¾ cups	sugar
6	eggs
2 cups	confectioners' sugar
2¼ cups	all-purpose flour
¾ cup	unsweetened cocoa
2 cups	chopped walnuts*

Glaze:

¾ cup	confectioners' sugar
¼ cup	cocoa
1½-2 tbsp	milk

Preheat oven to 350°F. Grease and flour a 10- or 12-cup Bundt Pan.

In large bowl beat butter and sugar until light and fluffy. Add eggs, one at a time, beating well after each addition. Gradually add confectioners' sugar; blend well. By hand, stir in remaining cake ingredients until well blended. Spoon batter into prepared pan; spread evenly.

Bake for 58–62 minutes.** Cool upright in pan on cooling rack for 1 hour; invert onto serving plate. Cool completely.

In a small bowl, combine glaze ingredients until well blended. Spoon over top of cake, allowing some to run down the sides. Store tightly covered.

*Nuts are essential for the success of the recipe.

**Since this cake has a soft tunnel of fudge, ordinary doneness test cannot be used. Accurate oven temperature and baking time are critical.

CINNAMON CROWN CAKE

3 cups	all-purpose flour
2 cups	sugar
3 tsp	baking powder
½ tsp	salt
1 cup	butter, softened
1 cup	milk
3	eggs
3 tsp	vanilla
½ cup	chopped nuts
½ cup	quick-cooking oats
½ cup	firmly packed brown sugar
2 tsp	cinnamon
½ cup	applesauce

Preheat oven to 350°F. Grease and flour a 10- or 12-cup Bundt Pan.

In large bowl, combine first eight ingredients; beat 3 minutes at medium speed. Spoon half of batter into prepared pan. Stir remaining ingredients into the other half of the batter. Spoon over batter in pan.

Bake 55–65 minutes until toothpick inserted in center comes out clean. Cool upright in pan 30 minutes; invert onto serving plate. Serve warm with ice cream.

COCOA RIPPLE CURRANT CAKE

½ cup	finely chopped nuts
½ cup	sugar
1½ tbsp	unsweetened cocoa
1 tbsp	cinnamon
1 cup	butter, softened
8 oz	cream cheese, softened
1½ cups	sugar
1½ tsp	vanilla
4	eggs
2¼ cups	all-purpose flour
1½ tsp	baking powder
½-1 cup	currants or raisins (optional)
½ cup	finely chopped nuts

Preheat oven to 325°F. Grease a 10- or 12-cup Bundt Pan; sprinkle with ½ cup nuts. Combine the ½ cup sugar with cocoa and cinnamon; set aside.

In large bowl, cream butter, cream cheese, 1½ cups sugar and vanilla until light and fluffy. Add eggs, one at a time, beating well after each addition. In medium bowl, whisk together flour and baking powder. Add gradually to creamed mixture until moistened. By hand, fold in currants or raisins and remaining ½ cup nuts. Spoon ⅓ of batter into prepared pan; sprinkle with ½ of cinnamon/cocoa/sugar mixture. Repeat with ⅓ more batter and cinnamon/cocoa/sugar mixture; end with final ⅓ of batter.

Bake for 65–70 minutes or until cake tests done. Cool in pan 10–15 minutes; invert on wire rack or serving plate to complete cooling. If desired, sprinkle with confectioners' sugar.

BUTTERSCOTCH RUM RIPPLE CAKE

1 cup	butter, softened
2 cups	sugar
5	eggs
1 cup	sour cream
3 cups	all-purpose flour
1 tsp	baking soda
1 tsp	salt
1 tsp	vanilla
1 tbsp	rum extract
3¾-oz pkg	instant butterscotch pudding
¾ cup	butterscotch ice cream topping
1	egg

Preheat oven to 350°F. Grease and flour a 10- or 12-cup Bundt Pan.

In large bowl, combine first 9 ingredients and beat 3 minutes. In small bowl, combine 2 cups of prepared batter, instant pudding, ice cream topping and egg; beat 1 minute. Spoon half of cake batter into prepared pan. Add half of the butterscotch batter. Marble the layers with a knife, using a folding motion. Repeat with remaining batters.

Bake for 1¼ to 1½ hours or until cake tests done. Cool in pan 10–15 minutes; invert on wire rack or serving plate to complete cooling. Top with Butterscotch Glaze and decorate with chopped nuts.

TEMPTATION FRUIT CAKE

16-oz pkg	glacé fruitcake mix or glacé cherry-pineapple mix, cut finely
1 cup	slivered almonds
1 cup	raisins
1 cup	currants
1 tsp	allspice
1 tsp	cinnamon
1 tsp	nutmeg
½ tsp	mace
½ cup	fruit juice (grape, orange, etc.)
¼ cup	molasses
2 tbsp	brandy flavoring or sherry
4	eggs
1½ cups	all-purpose flour
½ tsp	salt
¼ tsp	baking soda
⅔ cup	firmly packed brown sugar
½ cup	butter, melted

Preheat oven to 300°F. Grease and lightly flour a 10- or 12-cup Bundt Pan.

Mix all ingredients in large bowl until well blended. Pour batter into prepared pan.

Bake for 1½ hours or until cake tests done. Cool in pan 10–15 minutes; invert on wire rack or serving plate to complete cooling.

PECAN CAKE

1 cup	butter, softened
2 cups	sugar
½ tsp	salt
3	eggs
2 tsp	vanilla
5 cups	vanilla wafers (crushed coarsely)
1 cup	all-purpose flour
5 tsp	baking powder
2 cups	milk
1 cup	chopped pecans

Preheat oven to 350°F. Grease and flour a 10- or 12-cup Bundt Pan.

In large bowl cream butter, sugar and salt. Beat in eggs and vanilla. Combine crushed vanilla wafers, flour and baking powder in medium bowl. Add ½ of crumb mixture to butter mixture with 2 cups of milk. Fold in remaining crumb mixture and pecans.

Bake for 55–60 minutes or until cake tests done. Cool in pan 10–15 minutes; invert on wire rack or serving plate to complete cooling. Serve warm with simple Lemon Sauce.

RUTH'S POUND CAKE

1 cup	margarine
½ cup	butter
1 lb	confectioners' sugar, sifted
6	large eggs
1 tsp	vanilla
½ tsp	almond extract
¼ tsp	salt
3 scant cups	sifted cake flour
24	whole almonds (optional)

Preheat oven to 350°F. Grease and flour a 10- or 12-cup Bundt Pan.

Have margarine, butter and eggs at room temperature for at least 3 hours before baking. Whip margarine and butter in large bowl and add confectioners' sugar gradually until it is the consistency of whipped cream.

Add eggs, one at a time, beating after each addition. Add vanilla and almond extracts and salt. Add flour, 1 cup at a time. Pour into prepared pan.

Bake for about 1¼ hours or until cake tests done. Cool in pan 10–15 minutes; invert on wire rack or serving plate to complete cooling. Sprinkle with confectioners' sugar.

With almonds: In prepared pan, fasten whole almonds to sides of pan with dabs of butter before adding batter.

CHOCOLATE CROWN CAKE

1 cup	butter, softened
1¾ cup	sugar
4	eggs
3 cups	all-purpose flour
2 tsp	baking powder
½ tsp	salt
1 cup	milk
1½ tsp	vanilla
½ cup	chocolate syrup
½ tsp	baking soda

Preheat oven to 350°F. Grease and flour a 10- or 12-cup Bundt Pan.

In large bowl, cream butter and sugar. Add eggs, one at a time, beating well after each addition. In medium bowl, whisk together flour, baking powder and salt; add alternately with milk and vanilla to creamed mixture. Beat until light and fluffy. Place ¼ of batter in a small bowl; add chocolate syrup and baking soda to this. Pour chocolate batter into prepared pan. Pour remaining white batter on top of chocolate batter.

Bake for 55–60 minutes or until cake tests done. Cool in pan 10–15 minutes; invert on wire rack or serving plate to complete cooling. Top with Chocolate Glaze.

CARAMEL APPLE CAKE

2 cups	all-purpose flour
1¾ cups	firmly packed brown sugar
2 tsp	cinnamon
1 tsp	salt
1 tsp	baking powder
1 tsp	baking soda
¾ cup	butter, softened
1½ tsp	vanilla
3	eggs
2 cups	peeled, thinly sliced apples
1 cup	chopped nuts
½ cup	raisins

Glaze:

¼ cup	butter
¼ cup	firmly packed brown sugar
1½ cups	confectioners' sugar
1 tsp	vanilla
2-4 tsp	milk
2-3 tbsp	chopped nuts

Preheat oven to 350°F. Generously grease (using 1 tbsp solid shortening) and flour a 10- or 12-cup Bundt Pan.

In large bowl, blend all cake ingredients except nuts and raisins; beat 2 minutes at high speed. Stir in nuts and raisins. Spoon into prepared pan.

Bake 45–55 minutes until toothpick inserted in center comes out clean. Cool upright in pan 30 minutes; invert on to serving plate. Cool completely.

For glaze, melt butter in small saucepan. Stir in brown sugar; remove from heat. Add confectioners' sugar, vanilla and milk; blend well. Immediately spoon over cake. Sprinkle with nuts.

CHOCOLATE ZUCCHINI CAKE

2 cups	all-purpose flour
1 tsp	baking powder
1 tsp	baking soda
¼ tsp	salt
1 tsp	cinnamon
¼ cup	unsweetened cocoa
3	eggs
1½ cups	granulated sugar
½ cup	canola oil
¾ cup	buttermilk
½ lb	raw zucchini, coarsely shredded
1 tsp	vanilla
1 cup	coarsely chopped walnuts
½ cup	raisins

Preheat oven to 350°F. Generously grease and flour a 10- or 12-cup Bundt Pan.

In medium bowl, whisk flour with baking powder, baking soda, salt, cinnamon and cocoa; set aside.

In large bowl with electric mixer at high speed, beat eggs until very light and fluffy. Gradually beat in sugar until very fluffy and light in color. Gradually beat in oil. With mixer at low speed, beat in flour mixture alternately with buttermilk in two additions.

Drain zucchini well; fold in to flour mixture with vanilla, walnuts and raisins. Turn into prepared pan.

Bake 55–60 minutes, or until cake tests done. Cool in pan 10–15 minutes; invert on wire rack or serving plate to complete cooling. Sprinkle with confectioners' sugar when cooled, if desired.

FIG CARROT CAKE (for a 6-cup Bundt Pan)

1½ cups	all-purpose flour
1 cup	sugar
1 tsp	baking powder
1 tsp	baking soda
¼ tsp	cinnamon
¼ tsp	salt
⅔ cup	canola oil
2	eggs
1 tsp	vanilla
1 cup	finely shredded carrots
½ cup	finely shredded coconut
¾ cup	cut-up dried figs

Preheat oven to 350°F. Grease and flour a 6-cup Bundt Pan.

Place dry ingredients in mixing bowl; add oil, eggs and vanilla. Beat 2 minutes until well blended. Add carrots, coconut and figs. Pour batter into prepared pan.

Bake for 40–45 minutes or until cake tests done. Cool in pan 10–15 minutes; invert on wire rack or serving plate to complete cooling. Top with Vanilla or Lemon Glaze. (Can also be baked in a 12-cup Bundt Pan.)

MEXICAN CHOCOLATE CAKE (for Bundtlette Pan or Bundt Brownie Pan)

4	1 oz squares unsweetened chocolate
¾ cup	finely chopped walnuts
2 tsp	cinnamon
¼ cup	butter, softened
2	eggs
½ cup	firmly packed brown sugar
½ cup	sugar
2 cups	all-purpose flour
2 tsp	baking powder
½ tsp	baking soda
½ tsp	salt
1 cup	buttermilk
1 tsp	vanilla

Glaze:

½ cup	chocolate chips
¼ cup	boiling water
½ tsp	cinnamon
1 cup	confectioners' sugar

Preheat oven to 325°F. Grease and flour Bundtlette Pan or Bundt Brownie Pan.

Grate chocolate and shop nuts finely; combine with cinnamon in small bowl and set aside. In large bowl, cream butter and eggs; add sugars. Beat until smooth. Add chocolate mixture and blend. In medium bowl, whisk together flour, baking powder, baking soda and salt; add alternately with buttermilk to creamed mixture. Add vanilla.

Bake for 40–45 minutes or until cake tests done (less for Bundt Brownie Pan). Cool in pan 10–15 minutes; invert on wire rack or serving plate to complete cooling.

In blender, combine chocolate chips and boiling water and blend until smooth. Add cinnamon. Add confectioners' sugar, one heaping tablespoon at a time. Blend until smooth. Refrigerate 20 minutes or until desired consistency. Glaze cakes.

APPLE STREUSEL CAKE

Streusel:

¾ cup	sugar
3 tsp	orange-flavored instant breakfast drink mix
2 tsp	cinnamon

Cake:

3 cups	all-purpose flour
2 cups	sugar
3 tsp	baking powder
3 tsp	orange-flavored instant breakfast drink mix
½ tsp	salt
1 cup	canola oil
½ cup	water
2 tsp	vanilla
4	eggs
4	cups peeled, thinly sliced apples

Preheat oven to 350°F. Generously grease (using 1 tbsp solid shortening) and flour a 10- or 12-cup Bundt Pan.

In small bowl, combine streusel ingredients; set aside. In large bowl, combine all cake ingredients except apples. Beat 2 minutes at high speed. Pour ⅓ of batter (1⅔ cups) into prepared pan. Layer 2 cups apple slices over batter; sprinkle with half of streusel mixture. Repeat layers with another ⅓ of the batter, remaining apple slices and streusel mixture, ending with remaining batter.

Bake 65–75 minutes until toothpick inserted in the center comes out clean. Cool upright in pan 3 minutes; invert on to serving plate. Sprinkle with confectioners' and cinnamon and serve with ice cream, if desired.

GEORGE WASHINGTON'S CURRANT POUND CAKE

1½ cups	butter, softened
2¾ cups	sugar
6	eggs
1½ tsp	vanilla
5 cups	all-purpose flour
1½ tsp	baking powder
1 tsp	nutmeg
½ tsp	salt
1 cup	milk
11 oz	currants

Preheat oven to 350°F. Grease and flour a 10- or 12-cup Bundt Pan.

In large bowl, cream butter and sugar until light and fluffy. Add eggs, one at a time, beating well after each addition. Add vanilla; continue beating until smooth and fluffy. In medium bowl, whisk together flour, baking powder and salt. At slow speed, add dry ingredients to creamed mixture alternately with milk, beginning and ending with flour mixture. Beat only until combined. Stir in currants.

Bake for 1½ hours or until cake tests done. Cool in pan 10–15 minutes; invert on wire rack or serving plate to complete cooling. Sprinkle with confectioners' sugar.

GRANOLA HARVEST CAKE

1¾ cups	boiling water
1 cup	granola
8 oz	raisins
1 cup	sugar
½ cup	firmly packed brown sugar
1 cup	shortening
3	eggs
2½ cups	all-purpose flour
2 tsp	baking powder
1 tsp	baking soda
1 tsp	salt
1 tsp	nutmeg
1 tsp	cinnamon

Preheat oven to 375°F. Grease and flour a 10- or 12-cup Bundt Pan.

Pour boiling water over granola and raisins in medium bowl; cool to lukewarm. In large bowl, cream sugars and shortening thoroughly. Beat in eggs until well blended. In medium bowl, whisk together flour, baking powder, baking soda, salt and spices.

While blending at low speed, add flour mixture and granola mixture to creamed mixture, beginning and ending with dry ingredients. Pour batter into prepared pan.

Bake for 40–50 minutes until cake tests done. Cool in pan 10–15 minutes; invert on wire rack or serving plate to complete cooling. Top with Coffee, Spice or Basic Vanilla Glaze.

CHOCOLATE CHERRY CAKE

2 cups + 2 tbsp	all-purpose flour
1½ cups	sugar
1½ tsp	baking soda
¾ tsp	baking powder
¾ tsp	salt
½ cup	butter, softened
1 cup	buttermilk
¼ cup	maraschino cherry juice
2	eggs
2	1 oz squares unsweetened chocolate, melted
⅓ cup	maraschino cherries, cut-up
½ tsp	liquid red food coloring

Preheat oven to 375°F. Grease and flour a Bundtlette Pan or Bundt Mini-Loaf Pan.

Measure flour into large mixing bowl. Add sugar, baking soda, baking powder and salt; stir well to blend. Add butter and buttermilk. Beat 2 minutes at medium speed.

Add cherry juice, eggs and chocolate. Beat 2 minutes more. Stir in cherries and food coloring.

Bake for 30–35 minutes or until cake tests done. Cool in pan 10–15 minutes; invert on wire rack or serving plate to complete cooling. Top with Basic Vanilla Glaze, substituting cherry juice for the milk.

TOMATO SOUP CAKE

¾ cup	shortening
1½ cups	sugar
3	eggs
3 cups	all-purpose flour, divided
1 tbsp	baking powder
1 tsp	baking soda
1 tsp	cloves
1 tsp	cinnamon
1 tsp	nutmeg
10.7-oz can	tomato soup
⅓ cup	milk
1 cup	chopped nuts
1 cup	raisins

Preheat oven to 350°F. Grease and flour a 10- or 12-cup Bundt Pan.

Add ½ cup flour to the nuts and raisins in medium bowl and mix well. In large bowl, cream together shortening and sugar. Add eggs to creamed mixture and blend. In medium bowl, whisk together dry ingredients. Combine soup and milk in medium bowl. Add flour mixture to creamed mixture alternately with tomato soup mixture. Fold in raisins and nuts. Pour batter into prepared pan.

Bake for 50 minutes or until cake tests done. Cool in pan 10–15 minutes; invert on wire rack or serving plate to complete cooling. Top with Vanilla, Coffee or Spice Glaze.

HONEY SPICE CAKE

1 cup	hot water
1 tsp	instant coffee powder
4	eggs, separated
¾ cup	sugar
½ cup	canola oil
1 cup	honey
3 cup	all-purpose flour
½ tsp	salt
2 tsp	baking powder
1 tsp	baking soda
½ tsp	ground cloves
½ tsp	allspice

Preheat oven to 350°F. Grease and flour a 10- or 12-cup Bundt Pan.

In small bowl, mix hot water with instant coffee; set aside. In large bowl, beat egg yolks with sugar until creamy. Add oil and honey to creamed mixture, beating after each addition until mixture is smooth and creamy.

Combine flour with salt, baking powder, baking soda and spices in medium bowl. Add dry ingredients to egg/honey mixture alternately with coffee, mixing only until well blended. Do not over mix. In separate bowl, beat egg whites until stiff, but not dry. Fold egg whites into honey-egg batter. Pour batter into prepared pan.

Bake for 50 minutes or until cake tests done. Cool in pan 10–15 minutes; invert on wire rack or serving plate to complete cooling. Top with Brown Butter Glaze.

CHOCOLATE CHIP CAKE

⅔ cup	butter, softened
1¾ cups	sugar
3 cups	all-purpose flour
3½ tsp	baking powder
¾ tsp	salt
1⅓ cups	milk
1 tsp	vanilla
1 tsp	almond extract
1 cup	miniature chocolate chips
4	egg whites (½ cup)

Preheat oven to 350°F. Grease and flour a 10- or 12-cup Bundt Pan.

In large bowl, cream butter and sugar until light and fluffy. In medium bowl, whisk together dry ingredients; add alternately to creamed mixture with milk. Add vanilla and almond extract. Stir in chocolate chips.

In small bowl, beat egg whites until stiff peaks form. Gently fold into creamed mixture. Pour batter into prepared pan.

Bake for 50 minutes or until cake tests done. Cool in pan 10–15 minutes; invert on wire rack or serving plate to complete cooling. Top with Chocolate or Vanilla Glaze.

CHOCOLATE MACAROON CAKE

Coconut-Macaroon Filling:

1	reserved egg white
¼ cup	sugar
1 cup	grated coconut
1 tbsp	all-purpose flour
1 tsp	vanilla

Cake:

2 cups	all-purpose flour
1¾ cups	sugar
½ cup	unsweetened cocoa
1 tsp	salt
1 tsp	baking soda
2 tsp	vanilla
¾ cup	cold water
½ cup	shortening
½ cup	sour cream
4	eggs

(reserve 1 egg white for filling)

Preheat oven to 350°F. Grease and flour a 10- or 12-cup Bundt Pan.

Filling: In medium bowl, beat egg white at high speed until soft peaks form. Gradually add sugar; beat until stiff peaks form. By hand, stir in coconut, flour and vanilla; blend well. Set mixture aside.

Cake: In large bowl, combine all cake ingredients; blend at low speed until moistened. Beat 3 minutes at medium speed. Pour batter into prepared pan. Drop teaspoonfuls of the coconut filling over the chocolate batter.

Bake for 50–60 minutes or until cake tests done. Cool in pan 10–15 minutes; invert on wire rack or serving plate to complete cooling. Top with Chocolate or Orange Glaze.

ORANGE YOGURT POUND CAKE

6	eggs, separated
¼ tsp	cream of tartar
2 cups	sugar, divided
1 cup	butter, softened
1 tbsp	grated orange peel
2 tbsp	orange juice
3 cups	all-purpose flour
1 tsp	baking soda
¼ tsp	salt
8 oz	Mandarin orange yogurt

Preheat oven to 350°F. Grease and flour a 10- or 12-cup Bundt Pan.

In medium bowl, beat eggs whites with cream of tartar and ½ cup sugar until very stiff. In large bowl, cream butter with remaining 1½ cups sugar until light and fluffy. Beat in egg yolks, one at a time. Blend in peel and juice. In medium bowl, whisk flour together with baking soda and salt. Add to butter mixture alternately with yogurt. Stir until smooth and creamy. Thoroughly fold beaten egg whites into batter.

Bake for 50–55 minutes or until cake tests done. Cool in pan 10–15 minutes; invert on wire rack or serving plate to complete cooling. Sprinkle with confectioners' sugar, to top with Orange Glaze.

Lemon Yogurt Variation: Lemon peel and lemon juice can be substituted in place of orange peel and juice; substitute unflavored yogurt in place of Mandarin orange. Use Lemon Glaze.

CARROT CAKE

2½ cups	sugar
1 cup	canola oil
4	eggs, separated
5 tbsp	hot water
2½ cups	all-purpose flour
1 tsp	cinnamon
1½ tsp	baking powder
½ tsp	baking soda
¼ tsp	salt
1 tsp	nutmeg
1 tsp	cloves
1½ cups	grated raw carrots
1 cup	chopped pecans

Preheat oven to 350°F. Grease and flour a 10- or 12-cup Bundt Pan.

In a large bowl, combine sugar and oil. Beat in egg yolks; add water and beat well. In medium bowl, whisk together dry ingredients and add to egg mixture. Fold in carrots and nuts. In separate bowl, beat egg whites until stiff and fold into egg mixture.

Bake for 60–70 minutes or until cake tests done. Cool in pan 10–15 minutes; invert on wire rack or serving plate to complete cooling. Top with Vanilla or Cream Cheese Glaze.

Cakes from scratch

ORANGE CHOCOLATE MARBLE CAKE

1 cup	butter, softened
1½ cups	sugar
4	eggs, separated
2½ cups	all-purpose flour
2 tsp	baking powder
¼ tsp	salt
⅔ cup	milk
¼ tsp	grated orange peel
¼ tsp	orange extract
¼ cup	unsweetened cocoa
¼ cup	water

Preheat oven to 350°F. Grease and flour a 10- or 12-cup Bundt Pan.

In large bowl, cream butter; add sugar gradually, beating until fluffy. Beat in egg yolks, one at a time, until light and fluffy. In medium bowl, whisk together flour, baking powder and salt. Add ⅓ at a time to creamed mixture, alternately with milk, until blended. In separate bowl, beat egg whites until stiff peaks form; fold into batter. Spoon ½ of batter into another bowl; stir in orange peel and orange extract. Blend cocoa and water in a cup; fold that into batter in first bowl. Spoon batters into prepared pan, alternating layers of chocolate and white at least 2 times.

Bake for 50–60 minutes or until cake tests done. Cool in pan 10–15 minutes; invert on wire rack or serving plate to complete cooling. Top with Chocolate or Orange Glaze.

GRAHAM CRACKER CAKE

2⅔ cups	finely crushed graham crackers
⅔ cup	grated coconut
⅔ cup	chopped nuts
1⅓ tsp	baking soda
3 tbsp	shortening
⅔ cup	sugar
⅔ cup	firmly packed brown sugar
5	eggs, separated
1⅓ cups	sour cream
1½ tsp	vanilla

Preheat oven to 350°F. Grease and flour a 10- or 12-cup Bundt Pan.

In medium bowl, combine graham crackers, grated coconut, nuts and baking soda. In large bowl, cream shortening and sugars; add egg yolks and beat well. Add sour cream and crumb mixture alternately to creamed mixture. In a separate bowl, beat egg whites until stiff peaks form. Fold egg whites and vanilla into creamed mixture. Pour batter into prepared pan.

Bake for 50–55 minutes or until cake tests done. Cool in pan 10–15 minutes; invert on wire rack or serving plate to complete cooling. Top with Butterscotch Glaze or Hot Lemon Sauce.

WALNUT-BOURBON POUND CAKE

2 cups	finely chopped walnuts
½ cup	bourbon
3½ cups	all-purpose flour
1½ tsp	baking powder
½ tsp	salt
½ tsp	nutmeg
½ tsp	cinnamon
¼ tsp	ground cloves
8	eggs
2 cups	butter, softened
2 cups	sugar
1 tsp	vanilla
½ cup	bourbon

Preheat oven to 350°F. Grease and flour a 10- or 12-cup Bundt Pan.

In small bowl, mix together chopped walnuts and bourbon. Let stand. In medium bowl, whisk together flour, baking powder, salt and spices. Set aside. In small bowl, beat eggs until they are thick and light. In large bowl, cream butter with sugar until light. Beat in vanilla. Add beaten eggs, beating at low speed, then at high speed until mixture is thick and fluffy. Gradually beat in flour mixture just until combined. Stir in bourbon/walnut mixture.

Turn batter into prepared pan; spread with rubber scraper so that batter is slightly higher at sides and against tube. Place a 12″ square of parchment paper over pan. Bake 55–60 minutes. Cool in pan 10–15 minutes; invert on wire rack or serving plate to complete cooling.

Soak an 18″ square of cheesecloth in ½ cup bourbon. Wrap cake completely in the cheesecloth, then in foil. Store several days in an upright container. Just before serving, glaze with Coffee Glaze and garnish with nuts or sprinkle with confectioners' sugar.

Cakes from scratch

ORIGINAL GERMAN POUND CAKE

1 cup	butter
1 cup	sugar
1 cup	confectioners' sugar
4	eggs, separated
1 tsp	vanilla
1 tsp	almond extract
3 cups	all-purpose flour
2 tsp	baking powder
1 pinch	salt
1 cup	milk
48	whole almonds

Preheat oven to 350°F.

All ingredients must be at room temperature. In large bowl, cream butter. Sift the two sugars together and add gradually to butter. Add unbeaten egg yolks, one at a time, and beat until smooth. Mix in extracts.

In medium bowl, whisk flour, baking powder and salt together three times. Starting and ending with flour, add alternately with milk to creamed mixture. In a separate bowl, beat egg whites until stiff; fold into batter. Grease 10- or 12-cup Bundt Pan. Place 24 whole almonds in the bottom of the pan, securing with a dab of butter. Place another ring of remaining almonds on side of pan.

Pour batter into pan and bake for about one hour or until cake tests done. Cool in pan 10–15 minutes; invert on wire rack or serving plate to complete cooling. Sprinkle with confectioners' sugar.

LADY BIRD'S FAMOUS LEMON CAKE

¾ cup	butter, softened
1¼ cups	sugar
8	egg yolks
2½ cups	all-purpose flour
3 tsp	baking powder
½ tsp	salt
¾ cup	milk
1 tsp	vanilla
1 tsp	grated lemon peel
1 tsp	lemon juice

Preheat oven to 350°F. Grease and flour a 10- or 12-cup Bundt Pan.

In large bowl, cream butter and sugar until light and fluffy. In a separate bowl, beat egg yolks until light and lemon colored; blend into creamed mixture. In a medium bowl, sift together flour, baking powder and salt three times. Add the sifted ingredients to the creamed mixture in thirds, alternating with milk. Add vanilla, grated lemon peel and lemon juice. Beat two minutes. Pour batter into prepared pan.

Bake for one hour or until cake tests done. Cool in pan 10–15 minutes; invert on wire rack or serving plate to complete cooling. Sprinkle top with confectioners' sugar if desired.

GLUTEN FREE BLACKBERRY YOGURT CAKE

2 tbsp	butter, melted and cooled
1½ cups	gluten free all-purpose flour*
1 tbsp	baking powder
1 tsp	salt
1½ cups	white sugar
1 cup	butter
5	large eggs, room temperature
1 tbsp	lemon zest
2 tsp	vanilla extract
1¾ cups	yogurt
⅓ cup	milk
1½-2 cups	blackberries (cut in half if large)

Glaze: (optional)

1¼ cups	powdered sugar
2 tbsp	yogurt
4-5	crushed blackberries

Preheat the oven to 350°F. Melt butter and set aside to cool before prepping pan.

Combine gluten free flour, baking powder, and salt in bowl and set aside. Using a mixer with a paddle attachment, cream together sugar and butter until fluffy. Add eggs, one at a time, beating well after each addition. Stir in lemon zest and vanilla. Combine yogurt and milk in a medium bowl. Slowly add half of flour and yogurt-milk to sugar-butter mixture. Then add the other half of flour. Mix well and scrape sides of bowl. Fold in blackberries.

To prepare pan, brush cooled butter to lightly coat the details of the pan and evenly dust with gluten free flour (avoid forming clumps if possible). Pour batter into prepared pan and tap gently on counter to remove air bubbles. Bake for 40–50 minutes or until toothpick inserted in center of cake comes out clean. Let cool in pan for 10 minutes before unmolding. Cool cake completely before serving.

After cake has cooled, combine all glaze ingredients in bowl to the desired consistency and pour onto cake.

*Gluten Free Flour: We recommend using Bob's Red Mill® Baking 1:1 Flour, Cup 4 Cup Gluten Free All-Purpose Flour (not whole grain), or King Arthur Flour® Gluten Free All-Purpose Flour

Cakes from scratch

WHITE CHOCOLATE CAKE

¼ lb	white chocolate (almond bark)
½ cup	hot water
1 cup	sugar
1 cup	butter, softened
4	eggs
1 tsp	vanilla
2½ cups	all-purpose flour
1 tsp	baking soda
1 cup	buttermilk
4	egg whites
1 cup	chopped pecans
1 cup	coconut

Preheat oven to 350°F. Grease and flour a 10- or 12-cup Bundt Pan.

Melt the chocolate in ½ cup hot water. (It will take longer than regular chocolate.) In large bowl, cream sugar and butter until light and fluffy. Add the 4 eggs, one at a time, beating well after each addition. Add melted chocolate and vanilla.

In medium bowl, whisk flour and baking soda. Add alternately to creamed mixture with buttermilk, being careful not to over beat. Fold in stiffly beaten egg whites. Gently fold in pecans and coconut.

Bake for 45–50 minutes or until cake tests done.

Cool in pan 10–15 minutes; invert on wire rack or serving plate to complete cooling. Top with Vanilla Glaze, if desired.

THE DARKEST CHOCOLATE CAKE EVER

1 cup	butter, softened
2 cups	sugar
4	eggs
2½ cups	all-purpose flour
1 tbsp	baking soda
¼ tsp	salt
1 cup	buttermilk
¾ cup	unsweetened cocoa
⅔ cup	boiling water
2 tsp	almond extract

Preheat oven to 350°F. Grease and flour a 10- or 12-cup Bundt Pan.

In large bowl, cream butter with sugar until light and fluffy. Add eggs, one at a time, beating well after each addition. In medium bowl, whisk flour, baking soda and salt; add alternately with buttermilk to creamed mixture. Stir cocoa into ⅔ cup boiling water until dissolved. At low speed beat cocoa mixture and almond extract into batter. Pour into prepared pan.

Bake for 60–70 minutes or until cake tests done. Cool in pan 10–15 minutes; invert on wire rack or serving plate to complete cooling. Top with Vanilla Glaze.

Variation: 1 cup chopped nuts may be added if desired, or grease pan heavily and embed thinly sliced almonds over entire pan.

CHOCOLATE FONDANT CAKE

1 cup	butter, softened
1 cup	sugar
1 cup	firmly packed brown sugar
4	eggs
3	1 oz squares unsweetened chocolate, melted
1 cup	freshly cooked mashed potatoes or prepare instant mashed potatoes
1 tsp	almond extract
2 cups	all-purpose flour
1 tsp	baking soda
1 tsp	cream of tartar
1 tsp	salt
½ tsp	cloves
½ tsp	allspice
½ cup	sour cream
1 cup	chopped walnuts
1 cup	chopped pitted dates

Preheat oven to 350°F. Grease and flour a 10- or 12-cup Bundt Pan.

In large bowl, cream butter and sugars until light and fluffy. Add eggs, one at a time, beating well after each addition. Add chocolate, potatoes and almond extract.

In medium bowl, whisk flour with baking soda, cream of tartar, salt, cloves and allspice. Add to batter mixture alternately with sour cream. Fold in nuts and dates.

Bake in prepared pan for 60–65 minutes or until cake tests done.

Cool in pan 10–15 minutes; invert on wire rack or serving plate to complete cooling. Top with Vanilla or Brandied Chocolate Glaze.

ENCORE COFFEE CAKE

½ cup	shortening
¾ cup	sugar
1 tsp	vanilla
3	eggs
2 cup	all-purpose flour
1 tsp	baking powder
½ tsp	baking soda
½ pint	sour cream
6 tbsp	butter, softened
½ cup	firmly packed brown sugar
1 tsp	cinnamon
½ cup	chopped nuts

Preheat oven to 350°F. Grease a Bundtlette or Bundt Mini Loaf Pan.

Cream shortening, sugar and vanilla thoroughly. Add eggs, one at a time, beating well after each addition. In medium bowl, whisk flour, baking powder and baking soda.

Add to creamed mixture, alternately with sour cream, blending after each addition. Pour half of batter into prepared pan. In medium bowl, cream butter, brown sugar and cinnamon. Add nuts and mix well.

Sprinkle nut mixture over batter already in pan. Cover with remaining half of batter.

Bake at 350°F for about 35–40 minutes or until cake tests done.

Cool in pan 10–15 minutes; invert on wire rack or serving plate to complete cooling.

DATE BOURBON CAKE

2 cups	sugar
1⅓ cups	canola oil
4	eggs
3 cups	all-purpose flour
1½ tsp	baking soda
1 tsp	salt
1¼ tsp	nutmeg
1¼ tsp	cinnamon
1¼ tsp	allspice
1⅓ cups	buttermilk
1⅓ cups	chopped walnuts
1⅓ cups	chopped dates
1½ tsp	vanilla

Preheat oven to 350°F. Grease and flour a 10- or 12-cup Bundt Pan.

In large bowl, combine sugar, oil and eggs. Beat mixture until smooth and creamy.

In medium bowl, whisk dry ingredients; add alternately with buttermilk to creamed mixture. Mix until smooth. Stir in walnuts, dates and vanilla.

Bake for 50–60 minutes or until cake tests done. Cool in pan 10–15 minutes; invert on wire rack or serving plate to complete cooling.

Sprinkle with confectioners' sugar or top with Bourbon Syrup.

POPPY SEED COFFEE CAKE

1 cup	butter, softened
1½ cups	sugar
4	egg yolks
2½ cups	all-purpose flour
1 tsp	baking soda
2 tsp	baking powder
½ tsp	salt
1 cup	buttermilk
3 tbsp	poppy seed
½ tsp	almond extract
4	egg whites, beaten stiff

Preheat oven to 350°F. Grease and flour a 10- or 12-cup Bundt Pan.

In large bowl, cream butter with sugar until light and fluffy. Add eggs yolks, one at a time, beating well after each addition. In medium bowl, whisk flour, baking soda, baking powder and salt; add alternately with buttermilk to creamed mixture. Stir in poppy seeds and almond extract. Fold in stiffly beaten egg white.

Bake for 55–60 minutes or until cake tests done. Cool in pan 10–15 minutes; invert on wire rack or serving plate to complete cooling. Top with Lemon Glaze, if desired.

APPLE SWIRL CAKE

3-4	tart apples
3 tbsp	sugar
1 tsp	cinnamon
2 cups	sugar
1 cup	canola oil
4	eggs
¼ cup	orange juice
2 tsp	vanilla
3 cups	all-purpose flour
1 tbsp	baking powder
½ tsp	salt

Preheat oven to 325°F. Grease and flour a 10- or 12-cup Bundt Pan.

Peel, core and chop apples into small pieces. Mix together with 3 tbsp sugar and cinnamon. Set aside. In large bowl, combine sugar and oil; beat. Add eggs, orange juice and vanilla. In medium bowl, whisk flour, baking powder and salt; add to creamed mixture. Beat until smooth. Pour batter into prepared pan alternating with ½ apple mixture. Repeat. End with a layer of batter on top.

Bake for 60 minutes or until cake tests done. Cool in pan 10–15 minutes; invert on wire rack or serving plate to complete cooling. Sprinkle with confectioners' sugar.

Cakes from scratch

SPIRIT POUND CAKE

1 cup	butter, softened
2 cups	sugar
6	eggs, separated
3 cups	all-purpose flour
2 tsp	baking powder
⅛ tsp	ground nutmeg
¾ cup	Madeira, cream sherry or apricot brandy
¾ cup	finely chopped pecans

Preheat oven to 350°F. Grease and flour a 10- or 12-cup Bundt Pan.

In large bowl, cream together butter and sugar until light and fluffy. Add egg yolks, one at a time, beating well after each addition. In medium bowl, whisk together flour, baking powder and nutmeg; add alternately with the wine to the creamed mixture. Mix well after each addition. Blend in the chopped pecans.

In a separate bowl, beat egg whites until stiff. Fold into batter. Pour batter into prepared pan.

Bake for 50–60 minutes or until cake tests done. Cool in pan 10–15 minutes; invert on wire rack or serving plate to complete cooling. Sprinkle with confectioners' sugar before serving.

FRESH CRANBERRY NUT CAKE

1 cup	shortening
1½ cups	sugar
4	eggs
3 cups	all-purpose flour
2½ tsp	baking powder
½ tsp	salt
½ cup	milk
2 cups	chopped cranberries
1 cup	chopped pecans

Preheat oven to 350°F. Grease and flour a 10- or 12-cup Bundt Pan.

In large bowl, cream shortening and sugar until light and fluffy. Add eggs, one at a time, beating well after each addition. In medium bowl, whisk together flour, baking powder and salt. Add sifted dry ingredients alternately with milk to creamed mixture. Fold in cranberries and pecans. Pour into prepared pan.

Bake for 40–45 minutes or until cake tests done. Cool in pan 10–15 minutes; invert on wire rack or serving plate to complete cooling. Top with Orange Glaze.

Cakes
FROM MIXES

Cakes from mixes

DARK CHOCOLATE CAKE

1 pkg	dark chocolate cake mix, pudding included (approx 15.25 oz)
1 pkg	chocolate instant pudding mix (4-serving size)
1 cup	sour cream
⅓ cup	canola oil
½ cup	warm water
4	eggs
1½ cups	miniature semi-sweet chocolate chips

Preheat oven to 350°F. Grease and flour a 10- or 12-cup Bundt Pan.

In large bowl, combine all ingredients except chocolate chips. Beat 4 minutes. Fold in chocolate chips. Pour batter into prepared pan.

Bake for 50–60 minutes or until cake tests done. Cool in pan 10–15 minutes; invert on wire rack or serving plate to complete cooling. Sprinkle with confectioners' sugar.

PINEAPPLE UPSIDE-DOWN CAKE

6	maraschino cherries
20-oz can	crushed pineapple (reserve syrup)
⅓ cup	brown sugar
3 tbsp	melted butter
16-oz pkg	pound cake mix
1 tsp	lemon peel
1 tsp	vanilla

Preheat oven to 325°F. Grease and flour a Bundtlette Pan.

Coarsely chop cherries. Drain pineapple, reserving syrup. Combine cherries, ½ cup drained pineapple, brown sugar, melted butter and 3 tbsp pineapple syrup. Spoon into prepared pan.

Prepare pound cake mix according to package directions, using pineapple syrup for liquid. Stir in lemon peel, vanilla and remaining crushed pineapple. Spoon into pan.

Bake for 30–40 minutes or until cake tests done. Cool in pan 10–15 minutes; invert on wire rack or serving plate to complete cooling.

PUMPKIN PECAN CAKE

1 pkg	spice cake mix, pudding included (approx 15.25 oz)
1 cup	canned pumpkin
½ cup	canola oil
1 pkg	vanilla instant pudding mix (4-serving size)
3	eggs
1 tsp	cinnamon
½ cup	water
½ cup	chopped pecans

Preheat oven to 350°F. Grease and flour a 10- or 12-cup Bundt Pan.

In large bowl, combine first seven ingredients. Beat at medium speed for 5 minutes. Fold in chopped pecans. Pour batter into prepared pan.

Bake for 40–45 minutes or until cake tests done. Cool in pan 10–15 minutes; invert on wire rack or serving plate to complete cooling. Serve with whipped cream.

ORANGE DELIGHT CAKE

1 pkg	yellow cake mix, pudding included (approx 15.25 oz)
1 pkg	vanilla instant pudding mix (4-serving size)
½ cup	canola oil
¾ cup	orange juice
4	eggs
1 tbsp	butter flavoring (optional)

Filling:

¼ cup	sugar
2 tsp	cinnamon
½ cup	chopped nuts

Preheat oven to 350°F. Grease and flour a 10- or 12-cup Bundt Pan.

In large bowl, combine all ingredients and beat 5 minutes at medium speed. In separate bowl, mix together filling ingredients and set aside.

Sprinkle half of filling mixture in prepared pan, then fill one quarter full with batter. Sprinkle remaining filling mixture over batter in pan; add remaining batter.

Bake for 40–45 minutes or until cake tests done. Cool in pan 10–15 minutes; invert on wire rack or serving plate to complete cooling. Top with Orange Glaze.

CARAMEL BANANA CAKE WITH WALNUTS

1 pkg	white cake mix, pudding included (approx 15.25 oz)
4	eggs
¾ cup	water
⅓ cup	canola oil
1 cup	mashed bananas
¾ cup	chopped walnuts
1 pkg	butterscotch instant pudding mix (4-serving size)

Preheat oven to 350°F. Grease and flour a 10- or 12-cup Bundt Pan.

In large bowl, combine cake mix, eggs, water, cooking oil and bananas. Blend just until moistened, then beat 2 minutes at medium speed. Stir in walnuts. Set aside 1½ cups batter. Stir pudding into remaining batter until thoroughly blended. Pour into prepared pan. Top with reserved batter.

Bake about 50 minutes or until cake tests done. Cool in pan 10–15 minutes; invert on wire rack or serving plate to complete cooling. Sprinkle with confectioners' sugar.

Banana Surprise Cake: Substitute banana instant pudding mix in place of butterscotch and decrease amount of bananas to ½ cup.

BUTTERSCOTCH SPICE CAKE

1 pkg	spice cake mix, pudding included (approx 15.25 oz)
1 pkg	butterscotch instant pudding mix (4-serving size)
4	eggs
1 cup	water
⅓ cup	canola oil

Preheat oven to 350°F. Grease and flour a 10- or 12-cup Bundt Pan.

In large bowl, combine all ingredients and beat for 4 minutes. Pour batter into prepared pan.

Bake for 55–60 minutes or until cake tests done. Cool in pan 10–15 minutes; invert on wire rack or serving plate to complete cooling. Top with Vanilla or Butterscotch Glaze.

MOCHA NUT CAKE

1 pkg	yellow cake mix, pudding included (approx 15.25 oz)
1 pkg	chocolate instant pudding mix (4-serving size)
4	eggs
1 cup	sour cream
½ cup	cold coffee
⅓ cup	butter
½ cup	chopped walnuts

Preheat oven to 350°F. Grease and flour a 10- or 12-cup Bundt Pan.

In large bowl, combine all ingredients to moisten, then beat 2 minutes at medium speed. Pour batter into prepared pan.

Bake about one hour or until cake tests done. Cool in pan 10–15 minutes; invert on wire rack or serving plate to complete cooling. Sprinkle with confectioners' sugar.

PISTACHIO CAKE SUPREME

1 pkg	white cake mix, pudding included (approx 15.25 oz)
1 pkg	pistachio instant pudding mix (4-serving size)
4	eggs
⅓ cup	canola oil
1 cup	water
½ cup	sour cream
—	green food coloring
1 quart	pistachio nut ice cream

Preheat oven to 350°F. Grease and flour a 10- or 12-cup Bundt Pan.

In large bowl, combine cake mix, pudding mix, eggs, cooking oil, water and sour cream; beat 3 minutes. Add food coloring to desired color. Pour batter into prepared pan.

Bake for 40–50 minutes or until cake tests done. Cool in pan 10–15 minutes; invert on wire rack or serving plate to complete cooling.

Slice cake horizontally into 3 layers, placing bottom slice on serving plate. Soften ice cream and spread between layers. Place cake sections so that flutes are in line. Freeze until serving.

To serve: Sprinkle with confectioners' sugar, top with whipping cream and pistachio nuts or use a Chocolate Glaze.

BASIC LOW-FAT DREAM CAKE

1 pkg	yellow cake mix, pudding included (approx 15.25 oz)
2 oz	envelope whipped topping mix
4	eggs
1 cup	cold water

Preheat oven to 350°F. Grease and flour a 10- or 12-cup Bundt Pan.

In large bowl, combine cake mix, whipped topping mix, eggs and water. Blend until moist. Beat at medium speed for 3-4 minutes. Pour into prepared pan.

Bake for 40–45 minutes or until cake tests done. Cool in pan 10–15 minutes; invert on wire rack or serving plate to complete cooling. Glaze with Brandied Chocolate Glaze.

Variation 1: Substitute ¾ cup cold water plus 3 tablespoons frozen lemonade concentrate for 1 cup water. Add 1 tablespoon grated lemon peel. Top with Lemon Glaze.

Variation 2: Substitute 1 cup of orange juice for 1 cup water. Add 1 tablespoon grated orange peel. Top with Orange Glaze.

Variation 3: Substitute 1 cup ginger ale for 1 cup water. Add 1 tablespoon grated lemon peel. Top with Lemon Glaze.

EGGNOG CAKE

2 tbsp	butter, softened
½ cup	sliced almonds
1 pkg	yellow cake mix, pudding included (approx 15.25 oz)
½ tsp	nutmeg
2	eggs
1 cup	eggnog
2 tbsp	rum <u>OR</u>
1 tsp	brandy flavoring

Preheat oven to 325°F. Grease a 10- or 12-cup Bundt Pan with softened butter. Press almonds against the sides and bottom of pan; set aside.

In large bowl, combine cake mix, nutmeg, eggs, eggnog and flavoring. Beat at medium speed until smooth and creamy, about 4 minutes. Pour batter into prepared pan.

Bake for 50–55 minutes or until cake tests done. Cool in pan 10–15 minutes; invert on wire rack or serving plate to complete cooling.

Prick cake with thin skewer and top with Rum Syrup while cake is still warm.

SOUR CREAM BANANA PARTY CAKE

1 pkg	yellow cake mix, pudding included (approx 15.25 oz)
1 pkg	vanilla instant pudding mix (4-serving size)
3	eggs
½ cup	sour cream
¼ cup	canola oil
2	ripe bananas, peeled and cut into chunks (about 1½ cups)
¼ tsp	mace

Frosting:

3 oz	cream cheese, softened
3 tbsp	melted butter
½ tsp	grated orange peel
1 tbsp	orange juice
1½ cups	confectioners' sugar
—	banana slices, brushed with lemon juice, for garnish

Preheat oven to 350°F. Grease and flour a 10- or 12-cup Bundt Pan.

In large bowl, combine cake mix, pudding mix, eggs, sour cream, oil, bananas and mace. Stir to blend, then beat at medium speed for 5 minutes. Pour batter into prepared pan.

Bake for 50 minutes or until cake tests done. Cool in pan 10–15 minutes; invert on wire rack or serving plate to complete cooling.

For frosting, blend cream cheese with remaining ingredients in a medium bowl. Mix until smooth. Spread on top of cake and let drizzle down sides.

Garnish with banana slices and/or chopped walnuts. If desired, omit frosting and sprinkle cake with ½ cup sifted confectioners' sugar.

VERY BERRY LEMON CAKE

15-oz can	blueberries, drained OR
1 cup	blueberries, fresh or frozen
1 pkg	lemon cake mix, pudding included (approx 15.25 oz)
8 oz	plain yogurt or sour cream
4	eggs

Preheat oven to 350°F. Grease and flour a 10- or 12-cup Bundt Pan.

Rinse blueberries; drain well. In large bowl, combine cake mix, yogurt and eggs; blend at low speed until moist. Beat 2 minutes at medium speed. Fold the drained berries into mix. Pour batter into prepared pan.

Bake for 35–45 minutes or until cake tests done. Cool in pan 10–15 minutes; invert on wire rack or serving plate to complete cooling. Serve warm or cool with confectioners' sugar or whipped cream.

PAINTED PEACH CAKE

1 pkg	yellow, lemon or white cake mix, pudding included (approx 15.25 oz)
6 oz	cream cheese, softened
5	eggs
8 slices	well-drained sliced peaches (from a 15.25-oz can)
⅓ cup	red cinnamon candies (2-oz jar)

Glaze:

½ cup	sifted confectioners' sugar
1-2 tbsp	lemon juice

Preheat oven to 350°F. Grease and flour a 10- or 12-cup Bundt Pan.

In large bowl, combine dry cake mix, cream cheese and eggs. Blend until moistened and beat 2 minutes on medium speed. Spoon ⅔ of batter into prepared pan.

Arrange peach slices over cake batter, not touching sides of pan. Sprinkle cinnamon candies over peaches. Spoon remaining cake batter over candies.

Bake for 35–40 minutes or until cake tests done. Cool in pan 10–15 minutes; invert on wire rack or serving plate to complete cooling. Combine glaze ingredients in small bowl until desired consistency. Drizzle over warm cake. If desired, serve warm or cool with whipped cream or ice cream.

HARVEY WALLBANGER CAKE

1 pkg	yellow cake mix, without pudding (approx 15.25 oz)
1 pkg	vanilla instant pudding mix (4-serving size)
½ cup	canola oil
4	eggs
¼ cup	vodka
¼ cup	Galliano
¾ cup	orange juice

Preheat oven to 350°F. Grease and flour a 10- or 12-cup Bundt Pan.

In large bowl, combine all ingredients and beat for 4 minutes. Pour into prepared pan.

Bake for 45–50 minutes or until cake tests done. Cool in pan 10–15 minutes; invert on wire rack or serving plate to complete cooling. Sprinkle with confectioners' sugar or top with Orange Glaze.

SOUR CREAM COFFEE CAKE

1 pkg	yellow cake mix, pudding included (approx 15.25 oz)
1 pkg	vanilla instant pudding mix (4-serving size)
4	eggs
¾ cup	water
1 cup	sour cream
1 tsp	vanilla
¼ cup	canola oil

Filling:

¾ cup	sugar
2 tbsp	cinnamon
1 cup	finely chopped walnuts

Preheat oven to 350°F. Grease and flour a 10- or 12-cup Bundt Pan.

In large bowl, combine cake mix, pudding mix, eggs, water, sour cream, vanilla and oil; beat well. In separate bowl, combine sugar, cinnamon and nuts; set aside.

Sprinkle part of filling mixture in prepared pan to coat sides and bottom. Alternate layers of batter and remaining filling mixture in pan.

Bake for 45–50 minutes or until cake tests done. Cool in pan 10–15 minutes; invert on wire rack or serving plate to complete cooling. Wrap in foil immediately and allow to stand 2–3 days. Aging improves flavor.

DOUBLE LEMON CAKE

1 pkg	lemon or yellow cake mix, pudding included (approx 15.25 oz)
1 pkg	lemon instant pudding mix (4-serving size)
4	eggs
1 cup	water
⅓ cup	canola oil

Preheat oven to 325°F. Grease and flour a 10- or 12-cup Bundt Pan.

In large bowl, combine all ingredients and beat for 4 minutes. Pour batter into prepared pan.

Bake for 35–40 minutes or until cake tests done. Cool in pan 10–15 minutes; invert on wire rack or serving plate to complete cooling. Sprinkle with confectioners' sugar or top with a glaze, if desired.

INDIVIDUAL FLUTED SHORTCAKES

1 pkg	yellow cake mix, without pudding (approx 15.25 oz)
1 envelope	whipped topping mix
2	eggs
1 cup	cold water

Preheat oven to 350°F. Grease and flour 2 Bundtlette Pans.

In large bowl, combine cake mix, whipped topping mix, eggs and water. Blend until moistened. Beat at medium speed for 3–4 minutes. Divide batter between 2 prepared pans.

Bake for 15-20 minutes or until cakes test done. Cool in pan 10–15 minutes; invert on wire rack or serving plate to complete cooling. Top with your favorite fresh fruit.

PUMPKIN RUM CAKE

16-oz pkg	pound cake mix
⅓ cup	water
4	eggs
16-oz can	pumpkin
1½ tsp	pumpkin pie spice

Glaze:

1 cup	sugar
¼ cup	orange juice
—	2″ stick cinnamon
¼ cup	rum

Preheat oven to 325°F. Grease and flour a 10- or 12-cup Bundt Pan.

In large bowl, combine cake mix, water, eggs, pumpkin and pumpkin pie spice. Beat at medium speed for 3 minutes. Pour batter into prepared pan.

Bake for 55-60 minutes or until cake tests done. Cool in pan 10–15 minutes; invert on wire rack or serving plate and cool 20 minutes more.

Using a long-tined fork or skewer, punch holes in top of cake. In saucepan, combine sugar, orange juice and cinnamon stick; bring to boil. Remove cinnamon; stir in rum. Spoon orange mixture very slowly over cake, a small amount at a time, allowing cake to absorb sauce; continue until all syrup is used. Spoon any syrup that runs onto plate back over cake. Chill until serving time.

APPLESAUCE SPICE CAKE

1 pkg	spice cake mix, pudding included (approx 15.25 oz)
1 pkg	vanilla instant pudding mix (4-serving size)
4	eggs
½ cup	water
⅓ cup	canola oil
1 cup	applesauce

Preheat oven to 350°F. Grease and flour a 10- or 12-cup Bundt Pan.

In large bowl, combine all ingredients and beat for 4 minutes. Pour batter into prepared pan.

Bake for 55–65 minutes or until cake tests done. Cool in pan 10–15 minutes; invert on wire rack or serving plate to complete cooling. Top with Brown Butter, Spice or Coffee Glaze.

CHERRY CHOCOLATE MARBLE CAKE

1 pkg	cherry chip cake mix, pudding included (approx 15.25 oz)
1 pkg	vanilla instant pudding mix (4-serving size)
⅓ cup	canola oil
4	eggs
1 cup	water
—	red food coloring
2	1 oz squares unsweetened chocolate, melted

Preheat oven to 350°F. Grease and flour a 10- or 12-cup Bundt Pan.

Place first 5 ingredients in mixing bowl and beat 1 minute. Add enough red food coloring to make the batter a pink color. Beat 2 additional minutes. Place one half of the batter in a separate bowl and add melted chocolate to it. Alternate layers of chocolate and pink batter in prepared pan.

Bake for 50–55 minutes until cake tests done. Cool in pan 10–15 minutes; invert on wire rack or serving plate to complete cooling. Top with Chocolate Glaze.

DOUBLE CHOCOLATE FUDGE CAKE

1 pkg	chocolate cake mix, pudding included (approx 15.25 oz)
1 pkg	chocolate instant pudding mix (4-serving size)
4	eggs
1 cup	water
⅓ cup	canola oil
½ cup	finely chopped nuts (optional)

Preheat oven to 350°F. Grease and flour a 10- or 12-cup Bundt Pan.

In large bowl, combine all ingredients except nuts; beat for 4 minutes. Fold in nuts. Pour batter into prepared pan.

Bake for 55–60 minutes or until cake tests done. Cool in pan 10–15 minutes; invert on wire rack or serving plate to complete cooling. Dust with confectioners' sugar if desired, although it's delicious plain.

FRUITY SPICE CAKE

1 pkg	spice cake mix, pudding included (approx 15.25 oz)
1 pkg	butterscotch instant pudding mix (4-serving size)
4	eggs
1 cup	water
⅓ cup	canola oil
¼ cup	chopped nuts
¼ cup	chopped raisins
¼ cup	chopped glacé cherries
¼ cup	chopped glacé or dried pineapple

Preheat oven to 350°F. Grease and flour a 10- or 12-cup Bundt Pan.

In large bowl, combine the first 5 ingredients and beat for 4 minutes. Fold in chopped nuts, raisins and fruit. Pour batter into prepared pan.

Bake for 50–55 minutes or until cake tests done. Cool in pan 10–15 minutes; invert on wire rack or serving plate to complete cooling.

The fruit in this cake makes it very rich. However, it can be glazed or sprinkled with confectioners' sugar if a very festive appearance is desired.

HOLIDAY CRANBERRY CAKE

1 pkg	lemon cake mix, pudding included (approx 15.25 oz)
3 oz	cream cheese, softened
¾ cup	milk
4	eggs
1 tsp	mace
1¼ cups	ground cranberries
½ cup	ground walnuts
¼ cup	sugar

Preheat oven to 350°F.

In large bowl, combine cake mix, cream cheese, milk, eggs and mace. Beat 4-5 minutes at medium speed. Fold in ground cranberries and nuts. Grease a 10- or 12-cup Bundt Pan and sprinkle 1/4 cup sugar over surface. Pour batter into prepared pan.

Bake for 40 minutes or until cake tests done. Cool in pan 10–15 minutes; invert on wire rack or serving plate to complete cooling. Top with Lemon Glaze.

LEMON-CHEESE CAKE

1 pkg	yellow cake mix, pudding included (approx 15.25 oz)
¾ cup	apricot nectar
¼ cup	butter, softened
3	eggs

Filling:

2 8-oz pkgs	cream cheese, softened
½ cup	sugar
2 tbsp	lemon juice
1 cup	flaked coconut (optional)

Glaze:

2 cups	sifted confectioners' sugar
2 tbsp	lemon juice
2 tbsp	apricot nectar

Preheat oven to 350°F. Grease and flour a 10- or 12-cup Bundt Pan.

In large bowl, combine first 4 ingredients; beat as directed on cake package.

Spoon batter into pan. In small bowl, combine all filling ingredients; beat until smooth. Spoon filling over batter in pan, being careful not to let it touch sides of pan.

Bake for 50–55 minutes or until cake tests done. Cool in pan ½ hour; invert on wire rack or serving plate to complete cooling.

Combine all glaze ingredients and stir until smooth; drizzle over cake.

MALIBU BEACH BASKET CAKE

1¼ cups	dried pitted prunes
2	cups water (approx)
1	stick cinnamon
1 tsp	whole allspice
½ tsp	whole cloves
1 pkg	yellow cake mix, pudding included (approx 15.25 oz)
3	eggs
¼ cup	butter, softened
1 tbsp	grated orange peel

Orange Syrup:

⅓ cup	orange juice
½ cup	sugar

Preheat oven to 350°F. Grease and flour a 10- or 12-cup Bundt Pan.

Combine prunes, 1 cup water and spices in a small saucepan; simmer 15 minutes. Cool; drain and reserve juice; remove spices. Chop prunes to make 1 cup. In large bowl, combine cake mix, eggs, butter, orange peel and reserved juice plus water to make 1 cup. Mix as package directs, adding chopped prunes in the last minute of beating. Pour batter into prepared pan.

Bake for 55–60 minutes or until cake tests done. Cool in pan 10–15 minutes; invert on wire rack or serving plate to complete cooling.

For Orange Syrup, combine orange juice and sugar. Stir until sugar dissolves. Prick cake all over with fork. Slowly spoon Orange Syrup over cake, adding more as it absorbs. Cool before slicing.

SOUR CREAM CARDAMOM CAKE

4	eggs
12 oz	sour cream
1 pkg	yellow cake mix, pudding included (approx 15.25 oz)
1 tsp	cardamom, freshly ground

Filling:

½ cup	flaked coconut
½ cup	chopped pecans
½ cup	brown sugar
2 tbsp	all-purpose flour
2 tsp	cinnamon
¼ cup	butter, softened

Preheat oven to 350°F. Grease and flour a 10- or 12-cup Bundt Pan.

In large bowl, slightly beat eggs and combine with sour cream. Add cake mix and cardamom and beat 3 minutes. In separate bowl, combine filling ingredients and stir with fork until well mixed.

If desired, place 21 pecan halves with a dab of butter in bottom of prepared pan. Spread one third of the cake mixture into the pan. Sprinkle with one third of filling mixture. Continue alternating layers.

Bake for 45–50 minutes or until cake tests done. Cool in pan 10–15 minutes; invert on wire rack or serving plate to complete cooling. Sprinkle with confectioners' sugar.

ORANGE SPICE CAKE

1 pkg	spice cake mix, pudding included (approx 15.25 oz)
1 pkg	butterscotch instant pudding mix (4-serving size)
½ cup	water
⅓ cup	canola oil
½ cup	orange juice
4	eggs
½ cup	finely chopped nuts
½ cup	finely chopped raisins, floured

Topping:

2 cups	confectioners' sugar
—	juice and grated peel of 1 lemon
—	juice and grated peel of 1 orange

Preheat oven to 350°F. Grease and flour a 10- or 12-cup Bundt Pan.

In large bowl, combine cake mix, pudding mix, water, oil and orange juice. Blend well. Add eggs, one at a time, beating well after each addition. Beat for 4 minutes. Fold in nuts and floured raisins. Pour batter into prepared pan.

Bake for 55–60 minutes or until cake tests done. Cool in pan 10–15 minutes and invert on serving plate and prick top with a fork or skewer while still hot.

For the topping, blend ingredients well in medium bowl. Pour topping slowly over cake. Let cake stand about 10 minutes until topping is absorbed.

APPLESAUCE PUMPKIN CAKE

1 pkg	spice cake mix, pudding included (approx 15.25 oz)
16 oz	pumpkin pie filling (spiced)
½ cup	applesauce
3	eggs
½ cup	water

Preheat oven to 350°F. Grease and flour a 10- or 12-cup Bundt Pan.

In large bowl, combine all ingredients and beat 3 minutes. Pour batter into prepared pan.

Bake for 45–50 minutes or until cake tests done. Cool in pan 10–15 minutes; invert on wire rack or serving plate to complete cooling. Top with Spice, Vanilla or Brown Butter Glaze.

Note: If using regular canned pumpkin, decrease water by ¼ cup. Add 2½ tsp pumpkin pie spice and ½ cup brown sugar. Proceed as above.

PISTACHIO CAKE

1 pkg	yellow cake mix, pudding included (approx 15.25 oz)
4	eggs
1 cup	orange juice
⅓ cup	canola oil
1 pkg	pistachio instant pudding mix (4-serving size)
½ cup	chocolate syrup

Preheat oven to 350°F. Grease and flour a 10- or 12-cup Bundt Pan.

In large bowl, combine cake mix, eggs, orange juice, oil and pudding mix; blend at low speed for 1 minute, then beat at high speed 3 more minutes. Pour ⅔ of the batter into prepared pan.

Add chocolate syrup to remaining third of the batter and mix at medium speed until well blended. Pour over top of batter in pan. Marbleize by cutting through the batter with a knife.

Bake for about 1 hour until cake tests done. Cool in pan 10–15 minutes; invert on wire rack or serving plate to complete cooling. Top with Chocolate Glaze.

NEAPOLITAN POUND CAKE

8 oz	cream cheese, softened
4	eggs
1 pkg	white cake mix, pudding included (approx 15.25 oz)
¾ cup	milk or water
¾ cup	quick strawberry milk flavoring mix
1 tsp	vanilla
¾ cup	quick chocolate milk flavoring mix

Preheat oven to 350°F. Grease and flour a 10- or 12-cup Bundt Pan.

In large bowl, combine cream cheese and eggs. Beat until smooth. Add dry cake mix and milk or water. Blend until moistened. Beat as directed on package. Divide batter into thirds. Add dry strawberry milk flavoring mix to ⅓ of batter; pour into prepared pan. Add vanilla to another ⅓ of batter; pour over strawberry batter. Add dry chocolate milk flavoring mix to remaining ⅓ of batter; pour over vanilla batter.

Bake for 45–55 minutes or until cake tests done. Cool in pan 10–15 minutes; invert on wire rack or serving plate to complete cooling. Sprinkle with confectioners' sugar, or glaze if desired.

QUICK POPPY SEED CAKE

1 pkg	yellow cake mix, pudding included (approx 15.25 oz)
1 pkg	coconut cream instant pudding mix (4-serving size)
4	eggs
1 cup	water or orange juice
⅓ cup	canola oil
¼ cup	poppy seeds

Preheat oven to 350°F. Grease and flour a 10- or 12-cup Bundt Pan.

In large bowl, combine all ingredients and beat for 4 minutes. Pour batter into prepared pan.

Bake for 55–60 minutes or until cake tests done. Cool in pan 10–15 minutes; invert on wire rack or serving plate to complete cooling. Sprinkle with confectioners' sugar or top with glaze, if desired.

Variation: Cut poppy seeds to 2 tbsp and combine in small bowl with:

4 tbsp	instant cocoa
4 tsp	cinnamon
½ cup	chopped nuts

Fill prepared pan ⅔ full of batter; pour cocoa, cinnamon and nut mixture over batter; add remaining batter.

Bake for 50–55 minutes or until cake tests done. Cool in pan 10–15 minutes; invert on wire rack or serving plate to complete cooling. Top with Lemon Glaze.

CANADIAN PEANUT BUTTER CAKE

1 pkg	yellow cake mix, pudding included (approx 15.25 oz)
1½ cups	milk
½ cup	smooth peanut butter
2	eggs

Preheat oven to 350°F. Grease and flour a 10- or 12-cup Bundt Pan.

In large bowl, combine all ingredients and beat for 4 minutes at medium speed. Pour batter into prepared pan.

Bake for 40–45 minutes; cool in pan 10–15 minutes; invert on wire rack or serving plate to complete cooling. Glaze while cake is slightly warm.

ALMOND SHERRY CAKE

1 pkg	yellow cake mix, without pudding (approx 15.25 oz)
4	large eggs
¾ cup	cream sherry
¾ cup	vegetable oil
1 pkg	vanilla instant pudding mix (4-serving size)
½ tsp	nutmeg
¼ cup	sliced natural almonds, toasted

Streusel Filling:

⅓ cup	packed brown sugar
¼ cup	all-purpose flour
3 tbsp	cold butter
½ tsp	cinnamon
¾ cup	sliced natural almonds, toasted

Sherry Glaze:

2 cups	sifted confectioners' sugar
1/3 cup	butter, melted
1 tbsp	cream sherry
1-2 tsp	hot water

Preheat oven to 350°F. Grease and flour a 10- or 12-cup Bundt Pan.

In large bowl, combine cake mix, eggs, sherry, oil, pudding mix and nutmeg. Mix at low speed 1 minute, scraping bowl constantly. Mix at medium speed 3 minutes, scraping bowl occasionally (or beat by hand 5 minutes). Pour half of batter into prepared pan.

Combine all streusel ingredients except almonds in small bowl until crumbly. Stir in ¾ cup almonds. Sprinkle batter in pan evenly with streusel filling. Pour in remaining cake batter.

Bake for 45–50 minutes or until cake tests done. Cool on wire rack 15 minutes. Remove from pan; cool completely on rack.

Combine confectioners' sugar, melted butter and cream sherry in medium bowl. Stir in 1–2 tbsp hot water until glaze is of desired consistency. Brush cooled cake with sherry glaze; garnish with ¼ cup almonds.

CLASSIC HEAVENLY RUM CAKE

1 cup	chopped pecans or walnuts
1 pkg	yellow cake mix, without pudding (approx 15.25 oz)
1 pkg	vanilla instant pudding mix (4-serving size)
4	eggs
½ cup	cold water
½ cup	canola oil
½ cup	dark rum (80 proof)
—	Maraschino cherries
—	confectioners' sugar or whipped cream

Glaze:

¼ lb	butter
¼ cup	water
1 cup	granulated sugar
½ cup	dark rum (80 proof)

Preheat oven to 325°F. Grease and flour a 10- or 12-cup Bundt Pan. Sprinkle nuts over bottom of pan.

Mix all cake ingredients together in large bowl. Pour batter over nuts. Bake 1 hour. Cool in pan 10–15 minutes.

For glaze, melt butter in saucepan. Stir in water and sugar. Boil 5 minutes, stirring constantly. Remove from heat and stir in rum (optional).

Invert cake on serving plate and prick top with a fork. Drizzle and smooth glaze evenly over top and sides. Allow cake to absorb glaze. Repeat until all glaze is used. Decorate with whole maraschino cherries and a border of confectioners' sugar frosting or whipped cream. Serve with seedless green grapes, dusted with powdered sugar.

NUTTY CHERRY CHIP CAKE

1 pkg	cherry chip cake mix, pudding included (approx 15.25 oz)
½ cup	canola oil
4	eggs
2 pkgs	vanilla instant pudding mix (4-serving size)
1 cup	buttermilk
1 cup	angel flake coconut
1 cup	finely chopped pecans

Preheat oven to 350°F. Grease and flour a 10- or 12-cup Bundt Pan.

In large bowl, combine cake mix, oil, eggs, instant pudding and buttermilk; beat at medium speed 4-5 minutes. Fold in coconut and pecans. Pour batter into prepared pan.

Bake for 65 minutes or until cake tests done. Cool in pan 10–15 minutes; invert on wire rack or serving plate to complete cooling. Sprinkle with confectioners' sugar.

DEVILISH CHOCOLATE RUM CAKE

1 pkg	chocolate cake mix, without pudding (approx 15.25 oz)
1 pkg	chocolate instant pudding mix (4-serving size)
4	eggs
½ cup	dark rum (80 proof)
½ cup	cold water
½ cup	canola oil
½ cup	slivered almonds (optional)

Filling:

1½ cups	cold milk
½ cup	dark rum (80 proof)
1 pkg	chocolate instant pudding mix (4-serving size)
1 envelope	whipped topping mix

Preheat oven to 350°F. Grease and flour a 10- or 12-cup Bundt Pan.

Combine all cake ingredients in large bowl. Blend well, the beat at medium speed 2 minutes. Turn into prepared pan.

Bake 50 minutes or until cake tests done. Do not under bake. Cool in pan 10 minutes, remove from pan and finish cooling on wire rack. Split in layers horizontally to make 3 sections.

Filling: Combine milk, rum, pudding mix and topping mix in a deep, narrow-bottomed bowl. Blend well at high speed for 4 minutes until light and fluffy.

Spread 1 cup filling between each layer and over the top of cake. Keep cake chilled. Serve cold. Garnish with chocolate curls (optional).

Breads
QUICK AND YEAST

SWISS CHEESE BREAD

12-oz can	beer OR
1½ cups	milk
½ cup	warm water
2 tbsp	sugar
1 tbsp	salt
2 tbsp	butter
8-oz pkg	pasteurized process Swiss or American cheese (not natural cheese)
5 cups	all-purpose flour
2 pkgs	active dry yeast

In large saucepan, warm the beer (or milk), water, sugar, salt, butter and cheese. (Cheese does not need to melt down completely.) Cool to lukewarm (120°F).

In large mixing bowl, combine 2 cups flour with yeast; add warm (not hot) cheese mixture. Beat 3 minutes. Gradually stir in remaining 3 cups of flour to make stiff dough. Knead on a lightly floured board until smooth and elastic, about 5 minutes. Place in greased bowl, turning to grease top. Cover; let rise in warm place until doubled in bulk, about 45–60 minutes.

Grease a 10- or 12-cup Bundt Pan. Punch down dough, shape into roll and place in prepared pan. Cover; let rise in warm place until doubled in bulk.

Preheat oven to 350°F. Bake about 45–50 minutes or until bread tests done. Invert on wire rack immediately to complete cooling.

SOUTHERN SALLY LUNN

1 cup	milk
¾ cup	butter
¼ tsp	sugar
½ cup	warm water
2 pkgs	active dry yeast
4 cups	all-purpose flour
¼ cup	sugar
1 tsp	salt
2	eggs
½ tsp	vanilla OR lemon extract

In small saucepan, scald milk with butter (heat to 180°F). Cool. In another bowl, add ¼ tsp sugar to warm water. Dissolve yeast in warm sugar-water.

Place milk, yeast and dry ingredients in large bowl; add eggs and extract and beat well. The mixture is thick and must be pushed down with a rubber spatula. Let rise in bowl until doubled in bulk. Beat well.

Grease a 10- or 12-cup Bundt Pan. Place in prepared pan and let rise until pan is almost full.

Preheat oven to 375°F. Bake for 25–35 minutes. Cool in pan 5-10 minutes; invert on wire rack to complete cooling.

TOMATO CHEESE BREAD

3¼ cups	all-purpose flour
2 tbsp	sugar
1 tsp	salt
1 tsp	caraway seed
2 pkgs	active dry yeast
¼ tsp	baking soda
10.7-oz can	tomato soup
½ cup	processed cheese spread
2 tbsp	butter
¼ cup	water
1	egg

In large bowl, combine 2 cups of flour, sugar, salt, caraway seed and yeast. In saucepan, combine soda, tomato soup, cheese spread, butter and water and heat until warm. Add to dry ingredients. Beat for 2 minutes. Stir in egg and remaining flour to form a stiff batter.

Cover and let rise until doubled in bulk. Grease a 10- or 12-cup Bundt Pan. Stir dough vigorously and pour into prepared pan. Cover and let rise in warm place until pan is three-quarters full.

Preheat oven to 350°F. Bake for 35–45 minutes or until bread tests done. Invert immediately on wire rack to cool. Brush with melted butter.

SPICY APPLE BREAD

1 cup	canned applesauce
1 cup	prepared mincemeat
1 pkg	active dry yeast
¼ cup	warm water
½ cup	milk, scalded (heated to 180°F)
1 tbsp	sugar
1 tbsp	shortening
1 tsp	salt
4 cups	all-purpose flour
½ cups	finely chopped nuts

In medium bowl, combine applesauce with mincemeat. In small bowl, combine yeast and warm water; let stand 5 minutes. In large bowl, combine scalded milk, sugar, shortening and salt. Stir until shortening is melted and cool to lukewarm.

Stir dissolved yeast into lukewarm milk mixture. Stir in applesauce mixture. Gradually beat in flour until dough is elastic. Stir in nuts.

Cover and let rise in warm place until doubled in bulk, about 1 hour. Grease a 10- or 12-cup Bundt Pan. Punch down dough and spoon into prepared pan. Let rise until doubled in bulk.

Preheat oven to 350°F. Bake for 40–45 minutes or until bread tests done. Invert immediately on wire rack to cool. Top with Vanilla Glaze or serve hot with butter.

100% WHOLE WHEAT BREAD

2 pkgs	active dry yeast
¼ cup	warm water
1 cup	milk, scalded (heated to 180°F)
¼ cup	shortening
¼ cup	firmly packed brown sugar
3 tsp	salt
1⅓ cups	lukewarm water
5-6 cups	sifted whole wheat flour
¼ cup	toasted wheat germ

In small bowl, dissolve yeast in warm water. Let stand 5 minutes. Scald milk in small saucepan; add shortening, sugar and salt. Cool and add lukewarm water. Add yeast.

Pour milk mixture into large bowl; add flour gradually, one cup at a time, beating well after each addition. Add wheat germ with last cup of flour. Invert on lightly floured board. Let rest 10–15 minutes. Knead for 10 minutes (this is a very important step).

Place dough in a greased bowl, turning to grease top; cover and let rise 1 to 1½ hours. Punch down and knead a few minutes; let rest another ½ hour covered on the bread board. Grease a 10- or 12-cup Bundt Pan. Form dough into a long roll and place into prepared pan. Let rise until pan is three-quarters full.

Preheat oven to 350°F. Bake for 40–50 minutes. Invert immediately on wire rack to cool.

APRICOT GLAZED RUM COFFEE CAKE

1 pkg	active dry yeast
¼ cup	lukewarm water
¾ cup	scalded milk (heated to 180°F), cooled to lukewarm
3 cups	all-purpose flour
1 cup	butter
¾ cup	sugar
5	eggs
1 tsp	salt
1 tsp	rum
—	grated peel of 1 lemon

Glaze:

1 cup	apricot jam fruit juice or rum

In medium bowl, dissolve yeast in warm water. Add milk. Beat in 1 cup flour. Let rise approximately 1½ hours.

Grease a 10- or 12-cup Bundt Pan. In large bowl, cream butter and sugar. Beat in eggs, one at a time. Add yeast mixture, remaining flour, salt, lemon peel and rum. Beat well. Pour into prepared pan. Let rise until doubled in bulk.

Preheat oven to 350°F. Bake for 50–60 minutes. Cool in pan for 5–10 minutes; invert on serving plate.

For glaze, pour jam through a sieve to remove solids. Heat in small saucepan and thin with fruit juice or rum. Pour over cake.

CHOCOLATE DATE-NUT BREAD

1 cup	sliced, pitted dried dates
¾ cup	boiling water
6 oz	semi-sweet chocolate chips
¼ cup	butter
⅓ cup	sugar
1	egg, beaten
1 tsp	vanilla extract
¾ cup	milk
2¾ cups	all-purpose flour
1½ tsp	salt
1 tsp	baking powder
1 tsp	baking soda
1 cup	coarsely chopped walnuts
—	walnut halves for garnish

Preheat oven to 350°F. In large bowl, combine the sliced pitted dates and boiling water. Set aside. Over a saucepan of hot (not boiling) water, melt chocolate chips with butter in a medium heat-safe bowl. Add sugar and mix well. Let this mixture cool slightly. Stir in beaten egg and vanilla.

Add the melted chocolate and egg mixture and milk to the date mixture, stirring until well mixed. Sift flour, salt, baking powder and baking soda into date mixture and stir until all flour is just moistened. Fold in chopped walnuts.

Grease and flour a 10- or 12-cup Bundt Pan and arrange walnut halves in the flutes in the bottom of the pan, securing with a dab of butter.

Pour batter into prepared pan and bake at for 65–75 minutes or until bread tests done. Cool 5–10 minutes in pan; invert on wire rack to complete cooling.

ALMOND RAISIN BREAD

1¼ cups	milk, scalded (heated to 180°F)
¾ cup	butter
½ cup	sugar
1 tsp	salt
1 pkg	active dry yeast
¼ cup	warm water
2	eggs
4 cups	all-purpose flour
½ cup	golden raisins
½ cup	blanched whole almonds
—	confectioners' sugar

In large bowl, add butter, sugar and salt to scalded milk. Let cool. In small bowl, dissolve yeast in warm water; add to milk mixture. Add eggs, one at a time, beating well after each addition; add flour and raisins.

Cover and let rise in warm place until doubled. Grease a 10- or 12-cup Bundt Pan; fasten almonds to sides of pan with a dab of butter. Arrange dough in pan. Let rise until doubled.

Preheat oven to 350°F. Bake for approximately 50 minutes or until bread tests done. Invert immediately on wire rack to cool. Sprinkle with confectioners' sugar.

GOLDEN CROWN SWEDISH COFFEE CAKE

2 pkgs	active dry yeast
½ cup	warm water
6 tbsp	butter, softened
¾ cup	sugar
3	eggs
½ cup	scalded milk (heated to 180°F), cooled to lukewarm
3¾ cups	all-purpose flour
1½ tsp	salt
½ cup	golden raisins
2 tsp	grated lemon peel
1 tsp	lemon extract
1 tbsp	butter, melted
3 tbsp	fine dry bread crumbs
—	whole blanched almonds
—	confectioners' sugar

In small bowl, dissolve yeast in warm water. In large bowl, cream butter and sugar until fluffy. Add eggs, one at a time, beating well after each addition. Add yeast and cooled scalded milk. Add flour and salt. Beat until smooth. Stir in raisins, lemon peel and lemon extract. Cover and let rise 1½–2 hours until doubled in size.

Brush a 10- or 12-cup Bundt Pan with 1 tbsp melted butter and sprinkle with bread crumbs. Place almonds in flutes in bottom of pan. Spoon dough into pan, cover and rise until doubled in size.

Preheat oven to 350°F. Bake for 25–35 minutes or until cake tests done. Cool in pan for 5–10 minutes; invert on wire rack to complete cooling. Sprinkle with confectioners' sugar.

Do not let yeast doughs rise more than double or they may fall, become coarse and open, and very dry when baked.

CRANBERRY NUT BREAD

3 cups	all-purpose flour
3 tsp	baking powder
½ tsp	baking soda
1 tsp	salt
½ cup	butter
⅔ cup	sugar
1	egg
¾ cup	milk
1 cup	prepared cranberry orange relish
1 cup	chopped pecans

Preheat oven to 350°F. Grease and flour a 10- or 12-cup Bundt Pan.

Whisk together flour, baking powder, baking soda and salt in medium bowl. In large bowl, cream butter and sugar until blended. Add egg to butter mixture and mix well. Add sifted dry ingredients and milk alternately to butter mixture; mix thoroughly. Stir in cranberry relish and pecans. Pour into prepared pan.

Bake for 40-45 minutes or until bread tests done. Cool in pan 10–15 minutes; invert on wire rack to complete cooling.

When cool, wrap bread tightly in plastic wrap or aluminum foil and store overnight before slicing.

CRUNCHY GRANOLA COFFEE CAKE

3 cups	all-purpose flour
2 pkgs	instant dry yeast
½ cup	granola
⅓ cup	sugar
½ tsp	salt
½ cup	milk
½ cup	water
¼ cup	shortening
2	eggs

Filling:

⅓ cup	sugar
⅓ cup	all-purpose flour
⅓ cup	sunflower nuts
1 tsp	cinnamon
3 tbsp	butter, melted

Combine 1 ½ cups flour, yeast, granola, sugar and salt in large bowl and mix well. In saucepan, heat milk, water and shortening until warm (shortening does not need to melt); add to flour mixture. Add eggs. Blend until moistened; beat 3 minutes. By hand, gradually stir in remaining flour to make a stiff batter. Cover; let rise in a warm place until light and doubled, about 45 minutes.

Combine all filling ingredients in medium bowl; mix well. Grease a 10- or 12-cup Bundt Pan and coat the inside with a portion of the filling mixture. Reserve remaining filling. Stir down batter and spread half of batter evenly into prepared pan. Sprinkle with reserved filling and top with remaining batter. Cover, let rise in a warm place until light, about 30 minutes.

Preheat oven to 375°F. Bake for 25 minutes or until bread cake tests done. Cool in pan 10–15 minutes; invert on wire rack or serving plate to complete cooling. Serve warm or cold.

PINEAPPLE MONKEY BREAD

20-oz can	crushed pineapple
¼ cup	butter
½ cup	firmly packed brown sugar
½ cup	cherry preserves
½ tsp	almond extract
½ tsp	cinnamon
3 cans	refrigerated butter flake biscuits

Preheat oven to 375°F. Grease a 10- or 12-cup Bundt Pan.

Drain pineapple well. Melt butter in medium saucepan and stir in brown sugar, cherry preserves, almond extract and cinnamon until blended.

Add drained pineapple. Spoon half of mixture into prepared pan. Arrange 1½ tubes biscuits on edge on top of fruit mixture. Layer remaining fruit mixture over biscuits. Top with remaining 1½ tubes biscuits.

Bake for 35 minutes or until it test done. Cool in pan 5 minutes; invert on wire rack or serving plate to complete cooling.

APRICOT-NUT BREAD

1 cup	dried apricot halves
1 cup	orange juice
2 cups	all-purpose flour
3 tsp	baking powder
½ tsp	baking soda
½ tsp	salt
¼ cup	butter
¾ cup	sugar
1	egg
½ cup	milk
1 cup	whole bran cereal
½ cup	slivered blanched almonds
2 tsp	grated orange peel

Preheat oven to 325°F. Grease and flour a 10- or 12-cup Bundt Pan.

Dice apricots into ¼″ pieces. Place apricots and orange juice in small saucepan over low heat and bring to boil; continue cooking 5 minutes. Remove from heat and cool.

Whisk together flour, baking powder, baking soda and salt in a medium bowl. Cream butter and sugar in large bowl.

Add egg and milk to butter mixture; mix until blended. Stir bran, almonds, orange peel and apricot mixture into creamed mixture; mix well. Add sifted dry ingredients to batter; blend until dry ingredients are moistened. Spoon into prepared pan.

Bake for 40–45 minutes or until bread tests done. Cool in pan on wire rack 5–10 minutes. Invert and cool completely.

When cool, wrap bread tightly in plastic wrap or aluminum foil. Store overnight before slicing.

JUBILEE COFFEE CAKE

¾ cup	sugar
¾ cup	chopped nuts
¾ tsp	cinnamon
2 16.3-oz pkgs	refrigerated biscuits
½ cup	butter, melted
12-oz jar	pure apricot preserves

Preheat oven to 350°F. Grease a 10- or 12-cup Bundt Pan.

In a small bowl, combine sugar, nuts and cinnamon. Sprinkle ¼ cup mixture into prepared pan. Cut biscuits into quarters and roll into balls.

Dip each ball in melted butter. Layer biscuit balls, cinnamon mixture and ½ cup preserves in pan.

Bake for 15 minutes or until it tests done. Invert on wire rack or serving platter; top with remaining preserves.

CHEESE COFFEE CAKE RING

16-oz pkg	hot roll mix
⅓ cup	warm water
⅓ cup	sugar
3	egg yolks
½ cup	sour cream
4 tbsp	butter, melted

Filling:

6 oz	cream cheese, softened
⅓ cup	sugar
1	egg
½ tsp	vanilla
—	grated peel of ½ lemon

Glaze:

10-oz jar	apricot jam, pressed through a sieve
¼ cup	chopped pistachio nuts

Dissolve yeast from package of hot roll mix in warm water. In large bowl, combine hot roll mix with ½ cup sugar.

In medium bowl, beat egg yolk until fluffy. Stir in sour cream, melted butter and yeast mixture. Gradually stir this mixture into flour mixture, beating until smooth.

Knead on a lightly floured board until soft and elastic (about 5 minutes). Cover and let rise in a warm place about 1½ hours, or until double in bulk. Punch down dough and knead for 5–10 minutes. Roll dough into circle about 18″ in diameter. Grease a 10- or 12-cup Bundt Pan.

Make filling: In medium bowl, beat cream cheese until fluffy; add ⅓ cup sugar, whole eggs one at a time, vanilla and lemon peel.

Fold dough in half and lay carefully over prepared pan. Open dough and fit into bottom and sides of pan, using care not to make holes. Pour in cheese filling. Lap top outside edges of dough carefully over filling; press down on ring to seal.

With kitchen shears, cut a cross in the part of dough covering the cone of the Bundt Pan; fold each triangle back over dough ring. Let rise to top of pan. Preheat oven to 350°F.

Bake for 40–45 minutes until it tests done. Invert on wire rack and cool in pan for 10 minutes; remove pan. Melt apricot jam in saucepan over low heat. Glaze cake using a pastry brush. Sprinkle top with pistachio nuts; complete cooling.

Note: In rising, the cheese sometimes seems to disappear into the dough, forming a tunnel in part of the loaf. This is typical of this type of coffee cake.

BUTTERMILK RAISIN BREAD

1½ cups	buttermilk
1 pkg	active dry yeast
¼ cup	sugar
2	eggs, beaten
½ cup	shortening, melted
1 cup	seedless raisins
5-5½ cups	all-purpose flour
1½ tsp	salt
½ tsp	baking soda
2 tbsp	wheat germ

In medium saucepan, heat buttermilk to warm (not hot) and transfer to a large bowl. Add yeast and sugar and stir to dissolve. Add beaten eggs, melted, cooled shortening and raisins. Whisk together flour, salt and baking soda in medium bowl. Add in thirds to yeast and egg mixture, beating well after each addition. Knead on lightly floured board until dough is soft and elastic.

Place dough in a greased bowl, brush with some softened shortening; cover and let rise until doubled in bulk. Place dough on board and let rest 15–20 minutes more.

Grease a 10- or 12-cup Bundt Pan. Coat pan with wheat germ. Shape dough into a roll to fit pan. Cover and let rise until double in bulk.

Preheat oven to 375°F. Bake for 30–35 minutes. Invert on wire rack to cool.

KUGLEHOPF (Austrian Coffee Cake)

1 pkg	active dry yeast
¼ cup	warm water
¾ cup	scalded milk (heated to 180°F) and cooled
¾ cup	butter, softened
⅔ cup	sugar
1 tsp	salt
4	eggs
4 cups	all-purpose flour
1¼ cups	currants or seedless raisins
¾ cup	slivered almonds
2 tbsp	grated lemon peel

In medium bowl, dissolve yeast in warm water. Add cooled, scalded milk to yeast. In large bowl, cream butter, sugar and salt until light and fluffy. Add eggs, one at a time, beating after each addition. Add yeast mixture.

Beat flour into yeast mixture until batter is glossy and smooth. Grease a 10- or 12-cup Bundt Pan. Chop ¼ cup of the nuts. Sprinkle into prepared pan. Combine remaining nuts, currants and lemon peel in a small bowl. Add to batter and blend in. Spoon batter into pan. Cover and let rise in warm place until batter comes to about ¼" from the top of the pan.

Preheat oven to 375°F. Bake for 40 minutes or until golden brown. Invert on wire rack to complete cooling. Sprinkle with confectioners' if desired.

BANANA DATE RING

4 cups	all-purpose flour
1⅓ cups	sugar
4 tsp	baking powder
1½ tsp	pumpkin pie spice
1 tsp	salt
¼ tsp	baking soda
1 cup	finely chopped walnuts
2	eggs
1 cup	milk
4 tbsp	butter, melted
3	large ripe bananas, peeled and mashed (1½ cups)
1 cup	chopped pitted dried dates

Preheat oven to 350°F. Grease and flour a 10- or 12-cup Bundt Pan.

Whisk flour, sugar, baking powder, pumpkin pie spice, salt and baking soda in large bowl; stir in walnuts. In separate bowl, beat eggs, stir in milk, melted butter, bananas and dates. Add to flour mixture; stir until just moist.

Bake for 1 hour or until it tests done. Cool in pan 10–15 minutes; invert on wire rack or serving plate to complete cooling.

LEMONY CHEESE RING

16-oz pkg	hot roll mix
1 cup	warm milk
1	egg
¼ cup	sugar
2 tbsp	butter, softened
½ tsp	salt

Filling:

1 cup	creamed cottage cheese
¼ cup	sugar
1 tbsp	all-purpose flour
2 tsp	butter, softened
2 tsp	lemon juice
1 tsp	lemon peel
2	egg yolks, beaten
2 tbsp	raisins

In large bowl, combine warm milk and yeast from hot roll mix; stir. Beat in egg, sugar, butter, salt and hot roll mix. Cover and let rise until double in bulk. Grease a 10- or 12-cup Bundt Pan.

To make filling, press cottage cheese through a sieve into medium bowl and then add sugar, flour, butter, lemon juice, lemon peel, egg yolks and raisins. Blend well.

Roll out dough to form a rectangle about 6″x20″. Spread with filling and roll up. Place in prepared pan, fitting ends together to form a perfect ring. Let rise until pan is ⅔ full.

Preheat oven to 350°F. Bake for 30–35 minutes until it tests done. Invert immediately on wire rack to cool.

POTICA

3½-3¾ cups	all-purpose flour
¼ cup	sugar
1 tsp	salt
1 pkg	active dry yeast
1 cup	milk
¼ cup	water
¼ cup	butter
2	egg yolks

Filling:

2 cups	ground walnuts
⅔ cup	sugar
6 tbsp	light cream
½ tsp	salt
½ tsp	vanilla
2 tbsp	butter
2 tbsp	fresh bread crumbs
2	egg whites

In large bowl, thoroughly mix 1¼ cups flour, sugar, salt and undissolved yeast. In small saucepan, heat milk, water and butter until warm. Gradually beat warm milk mixture and egg yolks into flour mixture; beat 2 minutes. Stir in remaining flour to make soft dough. Knead on lightly floured board until smooth. Place in greased bowl; turn dough to grease top. Cover, let rise in warm place until doubled.

To prepare filling, combine walnuts, sugar, cream, salt and vanilla in large bowl. Melt butter in saucepan over low heat; add bread crumbs and stir until golden. Add to nut mixture. In separate bowl, beat egg whites until stiff and fold into nut mixture.

Grease a 10- or 12-cup Bundt Pan. Punch down dough. Roll one half of dough into a 16″x9″ rectangle. Spread with half of the filling. Starting from the short end, roll up jelly-roll fashion and place in prepared pan. Repeat with remaining dough and filling and place second roll on top of the other roll in pan. Let rise until almost double, approximately 30–40 minutes.

Preheat oven to 375°F. Bake for 55–60 minutes or until it tests done. Invert immediately on wire rack to cool.

DATE FILLED POTICA

Follow Potica dough recipe (at left) and use the following filling:

2 cups	chopped walnuts
1 tsp	cinnamon
3 tbsp	sugar
½ cup	chopped pitted dried dates
¾ cup	milk
2	egg whites
1 cup	sugar

Make filling by blending walnuts, cinnamon, sugar, dates and milk in saucepan. Cook over medium heat, stirring until mixture thickens (about 10 minutes). Cool.

In medium bowl, beat egg whites until stiff; slowly add sugar, beating until meringue-like. Fold into cooled walnut mixture.

Grease a 10- or 12-cup Bundt Pan. Cut dough in half; roll half into 18" to 20" circle. Top dough with half of filling mixture. Roll up jelly-roll fashion. Place in prepared pan. Repeat with second half of dough; place second roll on top of first roll in pan. Let rise for approximately 30 minutes.

Preheat oven to 350°F. Bake for 50–60 minutes or until it tests done. Cool in pan for 5–10 minutes; invert on wire rack to complete cooling. Top with Vanilla Glaze.

INDIVIDUAL FLUTED PECAN ROLLS

16-oz pkg	hot roll mix, including ingredients required for mix
48	pecan halves
¾ cup	firmly packed brown sugar
½ cup	butter
1 tbsp	sugar
1 tbsp	water
½ tsp	cinnamon

Prepare hot roll mix as directed on box. Let rise in warm place until double in size (about 30 minutes).

Grease two 6-cavity Bundtlette Pans. Place 4 pecan halves in alternating larger flutes.

In a saucepan, combine brown sugar, butter, sugar, water and cinnamon. Heat until dissolved and spoon into prepared pans.

Pat down dough on floured board and divide into 12 pieces. Roll each piece into a 6" long pencil shape and press ends together to form a circle. Place in prepared pans. Let rise (about 20 minutes).

Preheat oven to 350°F. Bake for 15–20 minutes or until rolls test done. Immediately invert on wire rack to cool.

RAISIN RING COFFEE CAKE

16-oz pkg	hot roll mix
1 cup	very warm orange juice (120°F to 130°F)
1 tbsp	grated orange peel
½ cup	raisins
½ cup	firmly packed brown sugar
1 tsp	cinnamon
⅓ cup	chopped nuts

Glaze:

1 cup	confectioners' sugar
4 tsp	orange juice

In large bowl, dissolve yeast from hot roll mix in warm orange juice. Stir in orange peel, raisins and hot roll mix; blend well. Cover; let rise in warm place until light and doubled in size, 30-40 minutes. Generously grease a 10- or 12-cup Bundt Pan.

Combine sugar, cinnamon and nuts in a small bowl. On a floured surface, knead dough until no longer sticky; roll into a 20"x12" rectangle. Sprinkle with sugar mixture. Starting with the 20" side, roll up tightly. Seal edges. Cut into 16 slices. Form a ring of rolls by placing 8 slices, cut side down in larger flutes in bottom and partially up side of pan. Lay remaining 8 slices in pan. Cover; let rise again until light and doubled in size, 40–50 minutes.

Preheat oven to 350°F. Bake for 30–35 minutes or until cake tests done. Cool in pan for 5 minutes; invert on serving plate. Combine glaze ingredients; drizzle over warm cake.

CALYPSO JAVA BREAD

3 cups	packaged biscuit mix
¾ cup	firmly packed brown sugar
¼ cup	all-purpose flour
1 tbsp	instant coffee powder
½ cup	milk
1 cup	mashed bananas (2 bananas)
1	egg, beaten
1 cup	snipped dried dates
½ cup	chopped walnuts

Preheat oven to 350°F. Grease and flour a 10- or 12-cup Bundt Pan.

In large bowl, combine biscuit mix, brown sugar and flour.

Dissolve coffee powder in milk in small bowl; add to dry ingredients along with bananas and egg. Beat until blended. Stir in dates and nuts. Spoon into prepared pan.

Bake for 40–50 minutes or until bread tests done. Cool in pan for 5–10 minutes. Invert on wire rack to complete cooling.

"CAN'T MISS" CHEESY BREAD

2½ cups	all-purpose flour
2 tbsp	sugar
1 tsp	salt
2 pkgs	active dry yeast
½ cup	milk
½ cup	water
¼ cup	butter
1	egg
1 tbsp	sesame seed

Filling:

¼ cup	butter
½ tsp	Italian seasoning
¼ tsp	garlic powder
1 cup (4 oz)	shredded Cheddar cheese

Combine all filling ingredients in medium bowl. Mix well and set aside.

In large bowl, combine 1½ cups flour, sugar, salt and yeast; mix well. In saucepan, heat milk, water and butter until warm; add with egg to flour mixture. Blend until moistened; beat 2–3 minutes. Gradually stir in remaining flour to make a stiff batter.

Grease a 10- or 12-cup Bundt Pan; sprinkle with sesame seed. Put half of batter into pan; spread with filling. Top with remaining batter. If filling is not entirely covered, batter will cover during rising. Cover; let rise in warm place until doubled, about 1 hour.

Preheat oven to 350°F. Bake for 35–40 minutes or until bread tests done. Invert immediately on wire rack. Serve warm.

HOT PARSLEY BREAD

2 loaves	frozen bread dough
½ cup	butter, melted
2 tbsp	finely chopped parsley
½ tsp	minced onion

Thaw bread according to package directions. Grease a 10- or 12-cup Bundt Pan.

Knead two loaves together. Roll out on a floured surface to approximately an 18″x15″ rectangle. Add parsley and onion to melted butter, mixing well. Spread evenly over dough.

Roll up lengthwise. Seal edges and ends. Place dough, seam side down, in prepared pan. Let rise until doubled in bulk, approximately 30 minutes. With scissors, snip top of dough in evenly spaced intervals.

Preheat oven to 350°F. Bake for 20–30 minutes or until it tests done. Top may be covered loosely with aluminum foil to prevent over browning. Invert immediately on wire rack. Serve warm or cool.

KING'S BREAD

2 pkgs	active dry yeast
⅓ cup	lukewarm water
5-oz can	undiluted evaporated milk
5 cups	all-purpose flour
1 cup	butter, softened
¾ cup	sugar
1 tsp	salt
3	eggs, beaten
1 cup	chopped candied cherries
½ cup	chopped walnuts
1 tbsp	grated orange peel

Glaze:

1 cup	sifted confectioners' sugar
½ tsp	vanilla
1½ tsp	cream

In large bowl, dissolve yeast in water. Add milk and 1 cup of flour. Let rise for about 30 minutes or until doubled in bulk. Cream butter and sugar in medium bowl. Add salt and eggs. Beat into yeast mixture. Add remaining flour, beating well to keep smooth.

Knead on lightly floured board until smooth and elastic (about 10 minutes). Place in greased bowl, turning dough to grease top. Cover and let rise in warm place until doubled in bulk, about 1½ hours. Grease a 10- or 12-cup Bundt Pan.

Combine cherries, walnuts and grated orange peel. Pat dough to approximately 9″ to 10″ in diameter and top evenly with fruit mixture. Shape into a roll and fit into prepared pan. Cover; let rise about ½ hour or until pan is three quarters full.

Preheat oven to 350°F. Bake for 45–55 minutes or until it tests done. Invert immediately on wire rack to cool.

Combine all glaze ingredients until smooth. Drizzle over bread and decorate with additional candied fruit and nuts.

BRAN MUFFINS

3 cups	All-Bran® cereal
1 cup	boiling water
½ cup	shortening
1 cup	sugar
2	eggs
2½ cups	all-purpose flour
2½ tsp	baking soda
½ tsp	salt
2 cups	buttermilk

Preheat oven to 400°F. Grease a Bundtlette Pan.

Soak 1 cup of All-Bran in 1 cup boiling water in large bowl. Add shortening, sugar and eggs. Mix well.

Combine flour, baking soda and salt in medium bowl. Add alternately with buttermilk to egg-bran mixture. Mix in remaining 2 cups All-Bran. Spoon batter into prepared pan, filling each cup two-thirds full.

Bake for 15–20 minutes or until muffins test done. Invert immediately on wire to cool.

SWEDISH LIMPA

1 pkg	active dry yeast
¼ cup	warm water
—	grated peel from 2 oranges
1½ cups	water
¼ cup	molasses
⅓ cup	sugar
1 tsp	salt
3 tbsp	shortening
2 cups	rye flour
3 cups	all-purpose flour
1 cup	raisins (optional)
1 cup	candied citron (optional)

In small bowl, dissolve yeast in ¼ cup water. Place orange peel and 1½ cups water in a saucepan and bring to a boil; add molasses, sugar, salt and shortening. Transfer to large bowl and let cool until lukewarm; add yeast mixture.

Sift and mix flours; add gradually to contents of large bowl, beating well until smooth. Add raisins and citron, if using.

Knead on lightly floured board. Place in greased bowl, cover and let rise until doubled. Grease a 10- or 12- cup Bundt Pan. Shape into a roll and fit into prepared pan. Let rise until doubled.

Preheat oven to 350°F. Bake for 35–45 minutes. Cover with foil during the last 15 minutes of baking to prevent over browning. Invert immediately on wire rack to cool.

CARROT RAISIN BREAD

2½ cups	all-purpose flour
2 tsp	baking powder
1 tsp	baking soda
1 tsp	cinnamon
1 tsp	salt
1 cup	grated carrots
1 cup	golden raisins
½ cup	chopped walnuts
1 cup	firmly packed dark brown sugar
2	eggs
1 cup	milk
¼ cup	butter, melted

Preheat oven to 350°F. Grease a 10- or 12-cup Bundt Pan.

In medium bowl, whisk together flour, baking powder, baking soda, cinnamon and salt. In a second medium bowl, toss together carrots, raisins and chopped walnuts; mix in dark brown sugar.

In large bowl, beat eggs until foamy. Beat in milk and melted butter. Stir in carrot mixture, then flour mixture. Pour into prepared pan.

Bake for 50–60 minutes or until it tests done. Cool in pan for 5–10 minutes. Invert on wire rack to complete cooling.

SESAME-CRUSTED HEALTH BREAD

5-6 cups	all-purpose flour
2 pkgs	active dry yeast
½ cup	firmly packed brown sugar
1½ tsp	salt
½ cup	butter, softened
1½ cups	hot water
2	eggs
1 cup	wheat germ
¼ cup	sesame seeds

In large bowl, combine 2 cups of flour, yeast, brown sugar and salt. Stir to blend. Add butter and water; beat for 2 minutes. Add eggs and 1 more cup of flour; beat for 2 minutes. Stir in wheat germ. Gradually add remaining flour to form soft dough.

Knead on lightly floured board until dough is soft and elastic. Let rest on board for 20–30 minutes. Grease a 10- or 12-cup Bundt Pan and sprinkle with sesame seeds. Punch down dough and shape into roll to fit in pan. Let rise in warm place until about three-quarters full.

Preheat oven to 350°F. Bake for 35–40 minutes or until bread tests done; invert immediately on wire rack to cool.

FLUFFY ORANGE BREAD

2 pkgs	active dry yeast
2 tbsp	warm water
1 cup	orange juice, warm
1	egg
¼ cup	butter, melted
¼ cup	sugar
1 tsp	salt
¼ cup	honey
2 tbsp	grated orange peel
5 cups	all-purpose flour
1 tsp	vanilla

In small bowl, dissolve yeast in warm water. Blend orange juice, egg, butter, sugar, salt, honey and orange peel in large bowl; add yeast mixture. Add flour, 1 cup at a time, beating well after each addition. Add vanilla.

Knead dough until smooth and elastic. Place dough in a greased bowl, turning to grease the top. Let rise in warm place until doubled. Grease a 10- or 12-cup Bundt Pan. Punch down dough and place into prepared pan. Let rise until doubled.

Preheat oven to 350°F. Bake for 45–50 minutes or until bread tests done. Invert immediately on wire rack to cool.

CRANBERRY BREAD SWIRL

½ cup	milk, scalded (heated to 180°F)
¼ cup	butter
½ cup	sugar
1½ tsp	salt
2 pkgs	active dry yeast
½ cup	warm water
4⅔ cups	all-purpose flour
1	egg, beaten
2	egg yolks, beaten

Filling:

¾ cup	raisins
14-oz can	whole berry cranberry sauce
2 tbsp	grated orange peel

Stir butter, sugar and salt into scalded milk; cool until lukewarm. In small bowl, dissolve yeast in warm water. In large bowl combine flour, milk mixture, yeast, beaten egg and egg yolks; mix well. Beat until dough is smooth and elastic. Place in greased bowl, turning dough to grease top. Cover, let rise in warm place about an hour or until doubled in bulk. Grease a 10- or 12-cup Bundt Pan.

In medium bowl, combine raisins with cranberry sauce and orange peel. Roll ½ of dough into a rectangle approximately 20"x12". Spread with half of cranberry filling. Roll up dough jelly-roll fashion. Place into prepared pan, seam side down, ends slightly overlapping. Make a second roll with remaining filling and place seam side down on top of first roll, overlapping ends opposite those of first roll. Cover, let rise in warm place about 1 hour or until doubled. Preheat oven to 350°F. Bake for 60–70 minutes or until bread tests done. Cool in pan for 20 minutes; invert on wire rack to complete cooling.

Variation: Use 1 can of pie filling (cherry, blueberry, apple, etc.) instead of cranberry and raisin-orange filling.

CHEESE DATE BREAD

1 cup	milk, scalded (heated to 180°F)
1 cup	chopped pitted dates
2⅓ cups	all-purpose flour
¾ cup	sugar
4 tsp	baking powder
¼ tsp	baking soda
1 tsp	salt
1 cup	shredded Cheddar cheese (about ¼ lb)
1	egg, slightly beaten
1 tbsp	butter, melted

Preheat oven to 325°F. Grease and flour a 10- 12-cup Bundt Pan. Combine dates and scalded milk in a small bowl; set aside to soak for 5 minutes.

In large bowl, whisk together flour, sugar, baking powder, baking soda and salt. Stir in cheese; set aside. Stir egg and butter into date mixture until combined. Add to dry ingredient mixture, stirring until fully incorporated. Mixture should be moist.

Transfer dough to prepared pan and bake for 35–45 minutes or until bread tests done. Cool in pan for 10 minutes. Invert onto wire rack to complete cooling.

Wrap bread tightly in plastic wrap or aluminum foil and store overnight before slicing.

SPICY MANDARIN MUFFINS

11-oz can	Mandarin oranges (cut each slice into 3-4 pieces)
1½ cups	all-purpose flour
½	cup sugar
1¾ tsp	baking powder
½ tsp	nutmeg
½ tsp	salt
¼ tsp	allspice
⅓ cup	butter, softened
½ cup	milk
1	egg, beaten
¼ cup	sugar
½ tsp	cinnamon
¼ cup	butter, melted

Preheat oven to 350°F. grease a Bundt Brownie Pan or Bundtlette Pan.

Drain Mandarin oranges thoroughly. Combine dry ingredients in large bowl. Cut in softened butter until mixture resembles coarse crumbs. Add milk and egg; stir just until dry ingredients are moistened. Gently stir in oranges.

Divide batter evenly into prepared pan. Bake for 15–20 minutes. Invert on wire rack. Combine ¼ cup sugar and ½ tsp cinnamon.

While hot, dip tops of muffins into melted butter, then roll in cinnamon-sugar mixture.

APPLESAUCE NUT BREAD

1 cup	sugar
1 cup	applesauce
1/3 cup	canola or vegetable oil
2	eggs
3 tbsp	milk
2 cups	all-purpose flour
1 tsp	baking soda
½ tsp	baking powder
½ tsp	cinnamon
¼ tsp	salt
¼ tsp	nutmeg
¾ cup	chopped pecans

Filling:

¼ cup	firmly packed brown sugar
½ tsp	nutmeg
¼ cup	chopped pecans

Preheat oven to 350°F. Grease and flour a 10- or 12-cup Bundt Pan.

In large bowl, thoroughly combine the sugar, applesauce, oil, eggs and milk. Whisk together flour, baking soda, baking powder, cinnamon, salt and nutmeg in medium bowl. Add to applesauce mixture and beat until well combined. Stir in ¾ cup pecans.

Pour half of batter into prepared pan. Combine brown sugar, cinnamon and remaining pecans in small bowl. Sprinkle filling evenly over batter; pour remaining batter on top.

Bake for 45–55 minutes. Cover loosely with foil after first 30 minutes of baking. Cool in pan 5–10 minutes; invert on wire rack to complete cooling.

EASY ITALIAN RING

16-oz pkg	hot roll mix, including ingredients required for mix
2-3 tbsp	butter, softened
1 cup	grated Parmesan cheese
1 tsp	paprika
1 tsp	Italian seasoning

In large bowl, prepare hot roll mix as directed on package. Cover and let rise ½ hour in warm place. Grease a 10- or 12-cup Bundt Pan.

On a lightly floured board, roll dough into a rectangle about 6"x20". Spread with butter. Combine cheese and spices and sprinkle over dough.

Roll up tightly and place in prepared pan. Let rise until double. Preheat oven to 350°F. Bake for 30–35 minutes or until it test done. Invert on a wire rack to complete cooling.

WALNUT COTTAGE BREAD

½ cup	butter, softened
1 cup	firmly packed brown sugar
2 tbsp	grated lemon peel
2	eggs
1¼ cups	creamed cottage cheese
3 cups	all-purpose flour
3 tsp	baking powder
1 tsp	baking soda
½ tsp	salt
1 cup	chopped walnuts
½ cup	golden raisins
½ cup	halved candied cherries
—	walnut halves and candied cherries for decoration
½ cup	maple syrup
1 tbsp	sugar

Preheat oven to 350°F. Grease and flour a 10- or 12-cup Bundt Pan.

In large bowl, cream butter and sugar until light and fluffy. Beat in lemon peel and eggs; blend in cottage cheese. Combine dry ingredients in large bowl and stir in fruit and nuts. Add to creamed mixture and combine until thoroughly blended.

Place walnut halves and cherries in bottom of prepared pan. Spoon batter in, careful not to disturb the design.

Bake for 45–55 minutes or until bread tests done. Immediately invert on serving plate. Heat syrup and sugar to 230°F. Spoon over hot bread. Cool before serving.

SHERRY RAISIN BREAD

3¾ cups	packaged biscuit mix
1	egg
1 cup	milk
2 tbsp	butter, melted
½ cup	sherry wine
½ cup	golden raisins

Preheat oven to 350°F. Grease and flour a 10- or 12-cup Bundt Pan.

Combine all ingredients until well blended. Spoon into prepared pan.

Bake for approximately 30–40 minutes or until it tests done. Invert on wire rack to complete cooling.

Salads
AND
Entrées

Salads

THREE FRUIT SALAD

6 oz	cream cheese, softened
1 cup	mayonnaise or salad dressing
¼ cup	lemon juice
¼ cup	sugar
2 cups	canned pineapple bits, drained
2 cups	canned Mandarin orange sections, drained and diced
1 cup	maraschino cherries, diced
1 cup	canned Royal Anne cherries, pitted and quartered
1 cup	chopped pecans
2 cups	whipping cream, whipped (or frozen dessert topping, thawed)

In large bowl, blend cream cheese, mayonnaise, lemon juice and sugar. Lightly mix in pineapple, orange sections, cherries, nuts and whipped cream.

Pour into a 10- or 12-cup Bundt Pan. Cover top tightly with freezer wrap; freeze.

To thaw: Unwrap pan and let stand in hot water 2–3 minutes. Invert on serving plate and thaw one hour in refrigerator.

To serve: Garnish salad with endive and fresh strawberries, if desired.

STRAWBERRY SOUR CREAM MOLD

2 6-oz pkgs	strawberry gelatin
2 cups	boiling water
4 10-oz pkgs	frozen strawberries, partially thawed
3	medium bananas, mashed
12 oz	sour cream

Dissolve gelatin in boiling water. Add strawberries and stir until completely thawed. Add bananas.

Pour half of mixture into a 10- or 12-cup Bundt Pan. Chill until set. (Keep remaining gelatin mixture at room temperature so it does not set up too rapidly.)

Spread sour cream evenly over chilled set gelatin. Spoon remaining gelatin mixture on top and chill until firm.

RED-WHITE-AND-BLUE MOLD

Red Layer:

3-oz pkg	strawberry gelatin
¼ cup	sugar
1 cup	boiling water
½ cup	cold water
1 cup	sliced strawberries

White Layer:

3-oz pkg	lemon gelatin
1 cup	boiling water
1 pint	vanilla ice cream, slightly softened

Blue Layer:

3-oz pkg	lemon, black cherry or grape gelatin
¼ cup	sugar
1 cup	boiling water
½ cup	cold water
1½ cups	fresh, frozen or drained canned blueberries, mashed

For Red Layer: In large bowl, dissolve strawberry gelatin and ¼ cup sugar in 1 cup boiling water. Add ½ cup cold water. Chill until thickened; stir in strawberries. Pour into a 10- or 12-cup Bundt Pan. Chill until set but not firm.

For White Layer: In another large bowl, dissolve 1 package lemon gelatin in 1 cup boiling water. Add ice cream, blending well. Chill until thickened. Spoon into Bundt Pan over red layer. Chill until set, but not firm.

For Blue Layer: In a third large bowl, dissolve remaining package of gelatin and ¼ cup sugar in 1 cup boiling water. Add ½ cup cold water; chill until thickened. Stir in blueberries and spoon into pan over white layer.

Chill overnight or until firm. Invert and garnish as desired.

GRAPE MOLD SALAD

3-oz pkg	lemon gelatin
1½ cups	boiling water
3 oz	cream cheese, softened
½ cup	whipping cream, whipped
6-oz pkg	strawberry gelatin
2 cups	boiling water
2 cups	hot grape juice
2 15.25-oz cans	fruit cocktail, drained

In large bowl, dissolve lemon gelatin in 1 ½ cups boiling water. Chill until slightly thickened. Fold in cream cheese and ½ cup whipped cream. Place in a 10- or 12-cup Bundt Pan and refrigerate until quite firm.

In another large bowl, dissolve strawberry gelatin in 2 cups boiling water. Add 2 cups hot grape juice. Refrigerate. When partially set, add drained fruit cocktail and pour over lemon gelatin layer in Bundt Pan. Refrigerate until firm.

Invert and serve.

MOLDED SALMON SALAD

3 envelopes	unflavored gelatin
5 cups	milk
5	egg yolks
2 tsp	salt
¼ tsp	pepper
14.75-oz can	salmon, drained and flaked
2 tsp	prepared mustard
6 tbsp	lemon juice
6 tbsp	chopped pimento
2 tbsp	chopped green olives
1 cup	diced celery

Soften gelatin in 1 cup milk. Beat egg yolks and add with remaining milk, salt and pepper to softened gelatin. Place in saucepan over low heat and stir until gelatin is dissolved. Remove from heat and chill until mixture begins to thicken.

In medium bowl, combine salmon, mustard, lemon juice, pimento, olives and celery and fold into gelatin mixture.

Pour into a 10- or 12-cup Bundt Pan and chill until firm. Serve with sliced tomatoes and olives.

BASIC GELATIN DESSERT

2 6-oz pkgs	lemon gelatin
4 cups	boiling water
3¾ cups	cold water
2	bananas, sliced lengthwise
4	peach or pear halves
4	pineapple rings, cut in half

In large bowl, dissolve gelatin in boiling water; add cold water. (Do not use fruit juice as it gives a cloudy appearance to salad.) Pour gelatin into a 10- or 12-cup Bundt Pan; chill until slightly thickened. Press banana slices and peach or pear halves in large flutes, alternating with each other.

Press pineapple ring halves in narrow flutes. Cherries and additional fruits can be added to body of salad in center of mold, being careful not to disturb arranged fruit.

Chill until set. To unmold, dip pan in warm water; invert on serving plate. Garnish as desired.

TUNA OR CHICKEN SOUFFLÉ SALAD

2 envelopes	unflavored gelatin
½ cup	cold water
½ can	tomato soup
½ can	chicken consommé
¼ cup	lemon juice
1 tbsp	mustard
1 tbsp	prepared horseradish
1 tsp	salt
1 cup	mayonnaise
1 cup	canned tuna, drained OR
1 cup	cooked chicken, diced
1 cup	chopped celery
½ cup	chopped cucumbers
½ cup	chopped green pepper

Soften gelatin in cold water. In small saucepan, heat soup and consommé to boiling and add gelatin mixture and stir to dissolve. Stir in lemon juice, mustard, horseradish and salt. Cool until slightly thickened. Whip and add mayonnaise. Fold in tuna or chicken and vegetables.

Pour into Bundtlette Pan or Angel Cakes Mini Angel Food Pan and chill until set.

To unmold, dip pan in warm water and invert on cookie sheet. Transfer to serving plate with spatula.

SHORTCUT FROZEN SALAD

1 pkg	lemon instant pudding mix (4 serving size)
1 pint	frozen dessert topping, thawed
½ cup	mayonnaise or salad dressing
2 tbsp	lemon juice
14.5-oz can	fruit cocktail, drained
20-oz can	pineapple chunks, drained
1 cup	miniature marshmallows
¼ cup	chopped pecans

In large bowl, prepare pudding mix according to package directions. Blend in dessert topping, mayonnaise and lemon juice. Fold in the remaining ingredients and pour into a 10- or 12-cup Bundt Pan. Freeze until firm.

To unmold, dip pan in warm water and invert on a plate. Place back in freezer until ready to serve.

RASPBERRY-CRANBERRY WINE SALAD

6-oz pkg	raspberry gelatin
2 cups	boiling water
16-oz can	whole berry cranberry sauce
8-oz can	crushed pineapple, undrained
½ cup	Burgundy wine
⅓ cup	chopped walnuts
1	orange, sectioned
1	grapefruit, sectioned

In large bowl, dissolve gelatin in 2 cups boiling water. Stir in cranberry sauce, undrained pineapple, Burgundy and nuts. Chill until partially set.

Place the sections of oranges and grapefruit alternately in flutes of a 10- or 12-cup Bundt Pan. Add ½ cup of gelatin and let set. Add remaining gelatin. Chill until firm. Invert carefully onto serving plate.

Variation: ½ cup orange juice may be substituted for the Burgundy wine.

MOSAIC SALAD

3-oz pkg	lime gelatin
3-oz pkg	cherry gelatin
4 cups	boiling water
1 cup	cold water
6-oz pkg	lemon gelatin
½ cup	sugar
1 cup	pineapple juice
2 2-oz envelopes	whipped topping mix

Prepare lime and cherry gelatin separately, using 1 cup boiling water and ½ cup cold water for each. Pour each flavor into an 8″ square pan. Chill until firm or overnight.

In large bowl, combine the lemon gelatin, sugar and remaining 2 cups boiling water; stir until gelatin and sugar are dissolved. Stir in pineapple juice. Chill until slightly thickened.

Cut the lime and cherry gelatin into ½″ cubes. Prepare whipped topping mix as directed; blend with lemon gelatin. Fold in gelatin cubes. Pour into a 10- or 12-cup Bundt Pan and chill until set. To unmold, dip pan in warm water and invert on a dampened plate.

GOLDEN AVOCADO RING

20-oz can	pineapple chunks in juice
6-oz pkg	lemon gelatin
3 cups	boiling water
2 cups	white wine
1 tbsp	lemon juice
1	large avocado, diced
1 cup	sour cream
1 pinch	salt

Drain pineapple, reserving all juice. In large bowl, dissolve gelatin in boiling water. Stir in reserved pineapple juice, white wine, salt and lemon juice. Pour 2 cups mixture into bottom of a 10- or 12-cup Bundt Pan.

In medium bowl, combine drained pineapple chunks, avocado and sour cream; blend. Fold into thickened gelatin. Chill until firm.

HOLIDAY RIBBON RING

3-oz pkg	strawberry gelatin
1¼ cups	boiling water
16-oz can	whole berry cranberry sauce
3-oz pkg	lemon gelatin
1¼ cups	boiling water
8-oz pkg	cream cheese, softened
8-oz can	crushed pineapple, undrained
¼ cup	chopped salted pecans
2 3-oz pkgs	lime gelatin
2¼ cups	boiling water
2 tbsp	sugar
16-oz can	grapefruit sections, undrained

Cranberry Layer: In large bowl, dissolve strawberry gelatin in 1¼ cups boiling water. Add cranberry sauce, mixing well. Chill until partially set. Pour into a 10- or 12-cup Bundt Pan. Chill until almost firm; top with cheese layer.

Cheese Layer: In another large bowl, dissolve lemon gelatin in 1¼ cups boiling water. Add cream cheese and beat until smooth. Add pineapple (with syrup); chill until partially set. Stir in pecans. Pour over cranberry layer in mold. Chill until almost firm. Top with grapefruit layer.

Grapefruit Layer: In large bowl, dissolve lime gelatin and sugar in 2½ cups boiling water. Add grapefruit (with syrup); chill until partially set. Pour over cheese layer. Chill overnight.

BERRY-CHEESE MOLD

2 6-oz pkgs	lemon or strawberry gelatin
½ cup	sugar
4 cups	boiling water
3 cups	cold water
2 pints	strawberries, hulled and halved
2 8-oz pkgs	cream cheese, softened
2 tsp	vanilla

In large bowl, dissolve gelatin and sugar in boiling water. Add cold water. Chill 5 cups gelatin until thickened, leaving remaining gelatin at room temperature.

Add strawberries to thickened gelatin and pour into a 10- or 12-cup Bundt Pan. Chill until set, but not firm.

In large bowl, beat cream cheese until smooth; gradually add reserved gelatin and vanilla, beating until well blended. Spoon over gelatin in pan.

Chill overnight or until firm. Invert.

MOLDED FRESH CRANBERRY SALAD

2 6-oz pkgs	strawberry flavored gelatin
3 cups	boiling water
3 cups	cold water
5	medium oranges
16-oz pkg	fresh cranberries, coarsely chopped
2 cups	sugar
	lettuce leaves for garnish

Orange-Cheese Dressing:

8-oz pkg	cream cheese
⅓ cup	orange juice
2 tsp	grated orange peel
—	dash of salt

In large bowl, dissolve gelatin in 3 cups of boiling water; stir in 3 cups cold water. Refrigerate, stirring occasionally until mixture is slightly thickened.

Peel and chop oranges and place in large bowl; add cranberries and sugar, stirring until sugar is completely dissolved. Stir fruit mixture into thickened gelatin. Pour into a 10- or 12-cup Bundt Pan. Refrigerate until set.

Orange-Cheese Dressing: In a small bowl, at low speed, beat cream cheese and orange juice until smooth. Stir in orange peel and salt.

To serve, invert gelatin onto platter; garnish with lettuce leaves. Serve with Orange-Cheese Dressing.

SPAGHETTI FLORENTINE

16 oz	spaghetti, cooked and drained
10-oz pkg	frozen chopped spinach, thawed and drained
1 cup	chopped onion, sautéed in 1 tbsp butter
1 cup	Parmesan cheese
8 oz	chopped roasted red pepper
8 tbsp	butter, softened
4	eggs, lightly beaten
½ tsp	salt
½ tsp	nutmeg
—	pepper, to taste

Sauce:

3 cups	fresh mushrooms, sliced
2 tbsp	butter
24-oz jar	meatless spaghetti or marinara sauce

Preheat oven to 350°F. Grease a 12-cup Bundt Pan.

In large bowl, mix all ingredients together and place in prepared pan. Bake for 25 minutes. Cool 5 minutes before removing to a serving plate.

To make sauce, sauté mushrooms in 2 tbsp butter in large saucepan. Add spaghetti or marinara sauce and heat through.

Recipe can be cut in half for use in 6-cup Bundt Pan.

LAZY DAYS MEAT RING

4 lbs	ground beef
2 cups	soft bread crumbs
2	eggs
2 cups	beer
1 envelope	spaghetti sauce mix
3 tbsp	instant minced onion

Preheat oven to 350°F. Grease a 10- or 12-cup Bundt Pan.

In large bowl, combine ingredients in order given. Pack firmly into prepared pan. Bake for about 1¼ hours. Let stand 10 minutes. Invert onto serving plate.

Serve hot, garnished with ketchup, onion rings or cinnamon apple rings. Serve cold with cheese sauce.

CORNBREAD BUNDT WITH SAVORY CHEESE FILLING

Filling:

¼ cup	finely chopped onion
1	cored and seeded jalapeño
2 tbsp	finely chopped red and green pepper
6	minced garlic cloves
3 tbsp	softened unsalted butter
6½ oz	Boursin cheese
2 tbsp	softened unsalted butter
4 oz	shredded Cheddar or Manchego cheese
1	large egg
1 pinch	salt
1 pinch	pepper

Cake:

1½ cups	all-purpose flour
1½ cups	yellow cornmeal
3 tsp	baking powder
½ tsp	baking soda
1 tsp	salt
2 cups	buttermilk
6 tbsp	extra virgin olive oil or butter
2	large eggs
1¾ cups	whole kernel corn
1 cup	shredded Cheddar or Manchego cheese

Prepare a 10- 12-cup Bundt pan using a butter & flour method, or by using a baking spray which contains flour. Do not use cooking spray. Preheat oven to 350°F.

Filling: Sauté the onion, jalapeño pepper, bell peppers and garlic in 1 tablespoon of the butter. Cook until the onion is soft. Turn off heat and allow to cool. In a medium bowl, cream together the Boursin cheese, remaining 2 tablespoons butter, Cheddar or Manchego cheese, and 1 egg until smooth. Add the cooked onions and peppers. Mix well and season to taste with salt and pepper. Set aside.

Batter: Mix together the flour, cornmeal, baking powder, baking soda and salt in a large bowl. Add the buttermilk, oil or butter and 2 eggs and mix well. Mix in the corn and cheese and combine until fully incorporated. Pour half of batter into Bundt pan. Drop cheese mixture by the spoonful evenly in a circle around the pan, then top with remaining batter. Bake 50–55 minutes or until toothpick inserted 1″ into cake comes out clean. Note, this savory dish has a melted cheese center that is meant to be gooey. Allow cake to cool in pan 10 minutes, then invert onto a serving plate and enjoy warm. If reheating is necessary, cover with aluminum foil and place in a 300°F oven until warmed through.

BURGER IN A BUNDT

Crust:

2 cups	flour
2 cups	instant mashed potato flakes
¾ cup	butter, cut into small pieces
1 cup	milk

Filling:

2 lbs	lean ground beef
¾ cup	instant mashed potato flakes
½ cup	chopped onion
1 tsp	salt
½ tsp	pepper
½ cup	ketchup
2 tbsp	prepared mustard
2 10.75-oz cans	condensed Cheddar cheese soup

Preheat oven to 400°F.

In large bowl, combine flour and potato flakes. Cut in butter until crumbly. Stir in milk to form dough. Using back of spoon, form crust by pressing dough in the bottom and three-quarters up the sides of a 10- or 12-cup Bundt Pan.

In a very large sauté pan or Dutch oven, brown ground beef; drain. Stir in remaining filling ingredients; blend well. Spoon into crust.

Bake 30–40 minutes. Cool upright in pan 10 minutes; invert onto serving plate. Serve with additional ketchup and mustard, if desired.

Recipe may be halved for a 6-cup Bundt Pan. Decrease baking time by 10 minutes.

PARTY MEAT RING

3½ lbs	ground beef
2 cups	soft fine bread crumbs
1	egg, beaten
2 cups	milk
6 tbsp	minced onion
4 tsp	salt
½ tsp	pepper
4 tbsp	peanut butter
1 tbsp	horseradish
1 tbsp	ketchup

Preheat oven to 350°F. Grease a 10- or 12-cup Bundt Pan.

In large bowl, combine ingredients in order given. Pack firmly into prepared pan. Bake for 2 hours. Let stand 10 minutes; invert onto serving plate.

Garnish with cinnamon apple rings, broiled peach halves or ketchup and onion rings.

TURKEY IN THE BUNDT

6 cups	dry bread, cubed (unseasoned bread stuffing can be used)
2½ cups	cooked diced turkey
2½ cups	shredded Swiss cheese
1 tsp	instant minced onion
4	eggs, beaten
2½ cups	milk
¾ tsp	salt
¼ tsp	white pepper
⅛ tsp	poultry seasoning

Preheat oven to 350°F. Grease a 10- or 12-cup Bundt Pan.

Place 3 cups of bread cubes in bottom of prepared pan. Place turkey evenly over bread; then spread Swiss cheese over turkey layer. Sprinkle with minced onion. Top with remaining 3 cups bread cubes. Combine beaten eggs with milk and seasonings in small bowl; pour over mixture in pan.

Place Bundt Pan in another pan of water (1″–2″ deep) and bake for 1 hour. Remove from water bath and bake an additional 10 minutes or until a knife inserted in it comes out clean. Cool in pan 10 minutes.

With plastic spatula, lift turkey mixture away from edges of pan and remove to serving plate. Serve with buttered peas in center of ring. If desired, garnish plate with apple rings.

HAM RING

2½ lbs	lean ground ham
1 pound	lean ground beef
1 cup	soft bread crumbs
4	eggs
½ cup	evaporated milk
1 tbsp	instant minced onion
2 tbsp	prepared mustard
¼ cup	brown sugar
8-oz can	pineapple slices (optional)

Preheat oven to 350°F. Grease a 10- or 12-cup Bundt Pan.

In large bowl, combine ham, beef and bread crumbs. In small bowl, beat eggs together with milk, minced onion, mustard and brown sugar. Pour over meat mixture and combine thoroughly. If using, arrange pineapple slices in bottom of prepared pan. Press meat into pan.

Bake 1½ hours. Let stand 5 to 10 minutes. Invert onto serving plate.

SOUTH OF THE BORDER TAMALE CRESCENT RING

2 lbs	ground beef
½ cup + 1 tbsp	cornmeal
2 tsp	chili powder
1 tsp	salt
1 cup	chopped onion
1 cup	chopped olives
1 cup	ketchup
14.5-oz can	whole tomatoes
15-oz can	whole kernel corn
8-oz can	tomato sauce
2 8-oz cans	refrigerated crescent dinner rolls
2 cups	shredded Cheddar or American cheese

Preheat oven to 375°F.

In sauté pan, brown ground beef; drain. Stir in remaining ingredients except crescent rolls, cheese and 1 tbsp cornmeal. Simmer, uncovered, stirring occasionally, while preparing crust.

Separate crescent dough into 8 rectangles; firmly press perforations to seal. Place 6 rectangles, spoke-fashion, in 10- or 12-cup Bundt Pan, forming crust. Press to seal. Sprinkle bottom with 1 tbsp cornmeal and cheese. Spoon ground beef mixture over cheese. Cut each remaining crescent rectangle into 4 short strips; lay across top of filling spoke-fashion. Seal to outer and inner dough edges. Bake 25–35 minutes. Cool upright in pan 10 minutes; invert onto serving plate.

Recipe may be halved for 6-cup Bundt Pan.

INDIVIDUAL HAM MOLDS

1 lb	ground ham
1 lb	ground beef
1 cup	dry bread crumbs
1 cup	milk
¼ tsp	pepper
1 tbsp	minced onion
2	eggs, beaten
6	pineapple rings

Preheat oven to 350°F. Grease a 6-cavity Bundtlette Pan.

In large bowl, combine ham, beef, bread crumbs, milk, pepper, onion and eggs. Divide mixture equally and pat into the pan cavities.

Bake for 40 minutes. Remove from oven and add 1 pineapple ring on top of each individual ham mold. Bake for 10 minutes more. Remove from oven and loosen with spatula around center and sides. Invert onto cookie sheet; transfer to serving plate with spatula.

UPSIDE DOWN BURGER BISCUIT

2 lbs	ground beef
1½ cups	chopped onion
1½ cups	chopped celery
½ cup	quick-cooking oats
2 tsp	salt
1 tsp	chili powder
½ cup	ketchup
2 tsp	Worcestershire sauce
½ tsp	prepared horseradish, if desired
8-oz can	tomato sauce

Biscuit Topping:

1 can	refrigerated buttermilk or country style biscuits (8 count)
2 cups (8 oz)	shredded Cheddar cheese, divided
1 tbsp	chopped parsley
½ tsp	celery seed

Preheat oven to 375°F.

In sauté pan, brown ground beef; drain. Stir in remaining ingredients except biscuit topping. Spoon into 10- or 12-cup Bundt Pan.

Separate biscuit dough layers into 20 pieces. Layer 10 pieces over meat mixture. Sprinkle with 1½ cups cheese, parsley and celery seed. Top with remaining 10 biscuit pieces.

Bake 25–30 minutes. Cool upright in pan 10 minutes; invert onto serving plate. Sprinkle with remaining ½ cup cheese.

SPECIAL
Desserts

GALA RAINBOW ICE CREAM MOLD

½ gallon	vanilla ice cream
1 pint	lime sherbet
1 pint	lemon sherbet
1 pint	orange sherbet

Allow vanilla ice cream to soften. Make small balls of flavored sherbets about the size of a golf ball (these do not have to be perfect spheres). Place in freezer if they should begin to melt.

Stir softened vanilla ice cream to a creamy consistency. Spread about 1 cup in bottom of a 10- or 12-cup Bundt Pan. Place ⅓ of assorted sherbet balls in mold. Top with half of remaining vanilla ice cream. With flat side of a metal spoon, press mixture into pan.

Continue with remaining sherbet balls and ice cream, pressing firmly into place. Smooth top and cover with foil. Freeze.

To remove from mold, dip pan in warm water and invert on serving dish. Place back in freezer to firm up outside of mold. Slice to serve.

MINCEMEAT GINGER CAKE

14.5-oz pkg	gingerbread mix
1 cup	prepared mincemeat
½ cup	water
1	egg

Preheat oven to 350°F. Grease and flour a 6-cup Bundt Pan.

In large bowl, combine all ingredients and mix well. Bake for about 30 minutes or until cake tests done.

Cool in pan 5–10 minutes; invert on wire rack to complete cooling. Serve warm with whipped cream or Rum Syrup.

PEACH CUSTARD CAKE

¼ cup	butter
½ cup	brown sugar
2 tbsp	peach juice (from canned peaches)
2 15.25-oz cans	sliced peaches, reserve juice
¼ cup	chopped walnuts (optional)
15.25-oz pkg	yellow cake mix
1 pkg	vanilla instant pudding mix (4-serving size)
½ cup	canola oil
3	eggs
1 cup	peach purée
½ tsp	nutmeg

Preheat oven to 350°F. Grease a 12-cup Bundt Pan.

In small saucepan, melt butter with brown sugar. Add 2 tbsp peach juice. Pour into prepared pan. Place 2 peach slices in each wide section of Bundt Pan and 1 slice in each narrow section. Sprinkle with nuts, if desired.

Blend remaining peaches and juice in blender. Measure 1 cup of purée for cake batter. Combine cake mix, pudding mix, oil, eggs, purée and nutmeg in large bowl and beat 2–3 minutes. Pour on top of prepared peaches in Bundt Pan and bake for 45–50 minutes or until cake tests done.

Cool in pan 2 minutes; invert on serving plate. Serve warm. May be served with vanilla ice cream or whipped cream.

FROZEN EGGNOG PUDDING

2 15.25-oz cans	fruit cocktail
½ cup	maraschino cherries
6 oz	cream cheese, softened
⅛ tsp	salt
⅛ tsp	nutmeg
1 tsp	vanilla OR
½ tsp	rum and
¼ tsp	brandy extracts
1 cup	eggnog
1 cup	whipping cream
2 cups	miniature marshmallows (or about 24 big ones cut in small pieces)
—	red food coloring

Drain fruit cocktail. Drain and cut cherries in quarters. In large bowl, blend cream cheese with salt, nutmeg, extract and eggnog until smooth.

In a separate bowl, beat cream until stiff. Fold cream, marshmallows and drained fruit into cream cheese mixture. Tint with red food coloring, if desired.

Pour into a 10- or 12-cup Bundt Pan. Freeze 8 hours or overnight. Invert on cold platter. Decorate with whole maraschino cherries.

RASPBERRY ICE CREAM RING

4 pkgs	raspberry gelatin (4-serving size)
4 cups	boiling water
1 quart	vanilla ice cream
12-oz can	frozen pink lemonade concentrate, thawed
20-24 oz	frozen raspberries, thawed, reserving juice
½ cup	chopped pecans

In large heat-safe bowl, dissolve gelatin in boiling water; add ice cream, stirring until melted. Stir in lemonade and juice from raspberries.

Chill until partially set, and then fold in raspberries and pecans.

Pour into a 10- or 12-cup Bundt Pan. Chill until serving time.

PEAR CAKE WITH RUM SAUCE

15.25-oz can	pears, with juice
15.25-oz pkg	yellow cake mix
2	eggs
½ tsp	almond extract
—	jelly or jam

Glaze:

1 cup	confectioners' sugar
scant 1 tbsp	corn syrup
2 tbsp	milk
—	dash of salt
½ tsp	vanilla

Sauce:

1 pkg	vanilla instant pudding mix (4-serving size)
1½ cups	cold milk
¼ cup	dark rum (or to taste)
½ pint	whipped cream
—	toasted almonds (optional)

Preheat oven to 350°F. Grease and flour a 10- or 12-cup Bundt Pan.

For cake, purée canned pears with juice in blender for one minute. In large bowl, combine cake mix, eggs, puréed pears and almond extract and mix according to directions on cake mix package.

Bake for 40–45 minutes or until cake tests done. Cool in pan for 15–20 minutes. Invert on serving plate and spread cake with your favorite jelly or jam.

Blend glaze ingredients. Drizzle over jelly-coated cake.

For sauce: In medium bowl, mix pudding and milk thoroughly with whisk or spoon; let set. Add rum and fold in whipped cream. Serve sauce separately. Garnish with toasted almonds, if desired.

GLORIFIED RICE

¼ cup	cold water
1 envelope	unflavored gelatin
3 cups	cold, cooked rice
10-oz jar (1¼ cups)	maraschino cherries, drained and chopped
2	medium bananas, sliced and halved
20-oz can (2½ cups)	crushed pineapple, drained
2 cups	whipping cream, whipped
6 tbsp	sugar
½ tsp	salt
1 tsp	vanilla
½ tsp	almond extract

In small saucepan, sprinkle gelatin over water. Stir over low heat until gelatin is dissolved; cool. In very large bowl, combine remaining ingredients. Add gelatin; blend well.

Spoon into a 10- or 12-cup Bundt Pan; pack lightly. Chill until firm.

CANDIED FRUIT RICE CAKE

1½ cups	rice
6 cups	milk
1½ envelopes	unflavored gelatin
6 tbsp	rum
2	eggs, beaten
2 tsp	vanilla
1 cup	sugar
¾ cup	glacéed fruits or raisins

Caramel Sauce:

½ cup	sugar
2 tbsp	water

Cook rice and milk over water in double boiler for 45 minutes, stirring occasionally. Remove from heat. In small bowl, soften gelatin in rum. Add to rice with egg yolks, vanilla and sugar. Mix well. Stir in glacéed fruits.

To make caramel sauce, melt sugar and water in saucepan, stirring constantly until it becomes a deep golden color (it caramelizes). Pour into a 10- or 12-cup Bundt Pan and dip outside of pan into cold water for a second or two. Tip the pan so that the caramel runs all over the interior. When it stops running, set aside to cool.

When rice mixture has cooled, pour into Bundt pan and refrigerate to set. Invert and decorate with more glacéed fruit, if desired.

FROZEN DAIQUIRI SOUFFLÉ

8	eggs, separated
2 cups	sugar, divided
½ cup	lime juice
½ cup	lemon juice
—	grated peel of 2 lemons
—	grated peel of 2 limes
—	salt
2 tbsp	unflavored gelatin
½ cup	rum
2 cups	heavy cream
—	crushed pistachio nuts

In large bowl, beat egg yolks until light and fluffy. Add 1 cup sugar gradually; beat until smooth and light in color. Blend in lime and lemon juice, grated peel and a pinch of salt. Stir in large saucepan over low heat until it thickens. In small bowl, soak gelatin in rum. Stir gelatin and rum into hot custard until it is dissolved. Cool.

In medium bowl, beat egg whites until foamy. Add remaining 1 cup sugar gradually. Beat until stiff. In another bowl, whip cream until stiff.

Fold egg whites into custard; then fold in whipped cream. Pour into a 10- or 12-cup Bundt Pan and chill. Can be served refrigerated or frozen. To serve, top with pistachio nuts.

DELUXE CHEESECAKE

Crust:

1 cup	graham cracker crumbs
2 tbsp	sugar
¼ cup	butter, melted

Filling:

5 8-oz pkgs	cream cheese, softened
1¾ cups	sugar
3 tbsp	flour
1 tsp	grated lemon rind
¼ tsp	salt
1 tsp	vanilla
6	eggs
¼ cup	whipping cream

Preheat oven to 300°F.

Combine crust ingredients in a small bowl; lightly press into bottom of a 10- or 12-cup Bundt Pan.

In large bowl, combine all filling ingredients except eggs and cream; blend well. Add eggs; beat 2 minutes at high speed. Blend in cream. Spoon over crust.

Bake 65–75 minutes. Cool upright in pan 30 minutes. Chill in pan 2 hours; invert onto serving plate. Refrigerate.

SUMMER COOLER CAKE

3 pkgs	strawberry gelatin (4-serving size)
3 cups	boiling water
2 cups	cold water
2 15.25-oz cans	fruit cocktail, drained
1 packaged	8″ angel food cake

Dissolve gelatin in boiling water. Add cold water; cool about 10 minutes. Spread 1 cup of fruit cocktail in bottom of a 10- or 12-cup Bundt Pan. Pour in 1½ cups gelatin.

Brush crumbs off of angel food cake and place top side down, over fruit and gelatin in pan, pressing down lightly. Spoon remaining fruit cocktail around side of cake.

Pour remaining gelatin over cake. Chill until firm. Invert and serve with whipped topping, if desired.

CREATE-A-SUNDAE

9-oz box	chocolate wafer cookies, crushed
½ cup	butter, melted
1 quart (4 cups)	strawberry or cherry nut ice cream
1 quart (4 cups)	chocolate ice cream or chocolate variation, such as Rocky Road
1 quart (4 cups)	green peppermint ice cream
—	assorted ice cream toppings such as chocolate, butterscotch or strawberry
—	whipped cream or frozen whipped topping, thawed
—	toasted coconut
—	whole or chopped nuts
—	Maraschino cherries
—	sliced bananas
—	whole strawberries

Soften strawberry ice cream; spoon evenly into a 10- or 12-cup Bundt Pan. Freeze until firm.

Combine crushed cookies and melted butter; sprinkle half over frozen strawberry ice cream. Soften chocolate ice cream; spoon evenly over crumbs. Freeze until firm.

Sprinkle with remaining crumbs. Soften peppermint ice cream; spoon evenly over crumbs. Freeze until firm. Serve with assorted sundae accompaniments.

May be halved for a 6-cup Bundt Pan.

GRASSHOPPER CAKE

4	1 oz squares unsweetened chocolate
½ cup	boiling water
¼ cup	sugar
2¼ cups	all-purpose flour
1½ cups	sugar
3 tsp	baking powder
1 tsp	salt
½ cup	canola or vegetable oil
7	egg yolks
¾ cup	cold water
1 tsp	vanilla
7	egg whites
½ tsp	cream of tartar

Filling:

1 envelope	unflavored gelatin
¼ cup	cold water
⅓ cup	white crème de cocoa liqueur
½ cup	crème de menthe liqueur
2 cups	whipping cream

Preheat oven to 325°F. Grease a 10- or 12-cup Bundt Pan.

In medium bowl, combine chocolate, boiling water and ¼ cup sugar; stir until chocolate is melted. In large bowl, sift together flour, 1½ cups sugar, baking powder and salt.

Make a well in center of dry ingredients and add oil, egg yolks, cold water and vanilla in order given. Beat until very smooth. Stir the chocolate mixture into the egg yolk mixture. In another large bowl, beat egg whites with cream of tartar until very stiff peaks form.

Pour chocolate batter over entire surface of egg whites, folding gently to blend. Pour into Bundt Pan and bake for 50–55 minutes or until cake tests done. Cool in pan 10–15 minutes; invert on serving plate to complete cooling.

Filling: Soften gelatin in cold water. In small saucepan, heat together crème de cocoa and crème de menthe. Add softened gelatin. Stir until gelatin is dissolved. Cool. Whip cream, then fold in gelatin mixture. Refrigerate 15 minutes.

Split cooled cake crosswise into three layers. Spread ½ of filling between layers; place remaining ½ in center and on top of cake. Refrigerate until serving time.

Glazes,
SYRUPS
& SAUCES

Glaze is a favorite addition to enrich Bundt® cakes. It can be a thin or thick icing that is spooned over the top and flows down the flutes of the Bundt cake. It can be a basic glaze or varied with the addition of fruit flavors, spices or other ingredients.

BASIC GLAZE (VANILLA, RUM OR ALMOND)

2 cups	sifted confectioners' sugar	In medium bowl, combine sugar and butter. Add extract; add milk gradually to achieve desired consistency and stir until smooth.
1 tbsp	butter, softened	
1 tsp	vanilla, rum or almond extract	May be applied while cake is warm.
2-3 tbsp	milk	

For coffee cakes and breads, we suggest a thinner glaze:

1 cup	confectioners' sugar
1 tsp	butter, softened
½ tsp	vanilla, rum or almond extract
1 tbsp	milk

ORANGE GLAZE

2 cups	sifted confectioners' sugar	In medium bowl, combine sugar and butter. Add orange juice gradually to achieve desired consistency and stir until smooth. Stir in peel.
1 tbsp	butter, softened	
2-4 tbsp	orange juice	
1-2 tsp	grated orange peel	

LEMON GLAZE

2 cups	sifted confectioners' sugar	In medium bowl, combine sugar and butter. Add lemon juice gradually to achieve desired consistency and stir until smooth. Stir in peel.
1 tbsp	butter, softened	
2-4 tbsp	lemon juice	
1-2 tsp	grated lemon peel	

SPICE GLAZE

2 cups	sifted confectioners' sugar	In medium bowl, combine sugar, butter and spice. Add milk gradually to achieve desired consistency and stir until smooth.
1 tbsp	butter, softened	
½ tsp	pumpkin pie spice <u>OR</u> a combination of	
¼ tsp	cinnamon,	
⅛ tsp	cloves and	
⅛ tsp	nutmeg	
2-4 tbsp	milk	

CHOCOLATE GLAZE

2 cups	sifted confectioners' sugar	In medium bowl, combine sugar, cocoa powder and butter. Add vanilla; add milk gradually to achieve desired consistency and stir until smooth.
2 tbsp	cocoa powder	
1 tbsp	butter, softened	
½ tsp	vanilla	
2-4 tbsp	milk	

PEANUT BUTTER GLAZE

2 cups	confectioners' sugar	In medium bowl, combine sugar and peanut butter. Add milk gradually to achieve desired consistency and stir until smooth.
2½ tbsp	peanut butter (smooth or chunky)	
2-4 tbsp	milk	

BRANDIED CHOCOLATE GLAZE

2	1 oz squares semi-sweet chocolate	In small saucepan, melt chocolate with butter over low heat, stirring constantly until smooth. Remove from heat. In medium bowl, combine sugar, melted chocolate and brandy. Add milk gradually to achieve desired consistency and stir until smooth.
1½ tbsp	butter	
2 cups	sifted confectioners' sugar	
2 tbsp	brandy or kirsch	
1-3 tsp	milk	

BUTTERSCOTCH GLAZE

¼ cup	butter
¼ cup	firmly packed brown sugar
2 tbsp	milk
1 cup	confectioners' sugar
½ tsp	butterscotch extract

In saucepan combine butter, brown sugar and milk. Bring to full boil. Add confectioners' sugar and extract. Beat until smooth. Additional milk may be add to achieve desired consistency.

CREAM CHEESE GLAZE

3 oz	cream cheese, softened
1 tbsp	butter, softened
½ tsp	vanilla
1½ cups	confectioners' sugar
2-3 tbsp	milk

In medium bowl, combine cream cheese, butter and vanilla; beat until smooth. Add sugar; add milk gradually to achieve desired consistency. Beat until smooth.

BROWN BUTTER GLAZE

¼	cup butter
—	juice of ½ orange
2 cups	confectioners' sugar

In medium saucepan, melt butter until golden brown; add orange juice. Cool. Add melted butter to sugar and stir until smooth.

COFFEE GLAZE

2 tsp	instant coffee granules
scant 3 tbsp	hot milk
2 cups	confectioners' sugar
1 tbsp	butter, softened

Dissolve instant coffee in hot milk. In medium bowl, combine sugar and butter. Add milk gradually to achieve desired consistency and stir until smooth.

BOURBON SYRUP

1 cup	sugar
½ cup	water
1 tsp	butter
½ tsp	vanilla
½ oz	bourbon

In medium saucepan, boil sugar and water 5 minutes. Add remaining ingredients. Cook until it's a syrupy mixture.

RUM SYRUP

1 cup	sugar
½ cup	water
1 tsp	butter
½ tsp	vanilla
½ oz	rum

In medium saucepan, boil sugar and water 5 minutes. Add remaining ingredients. Cook until it's a syrupy mixture.

Sauces introduce a new flavor, compliment an existing flavor and generally add color, taste and texture to Bundt cakes. Canned pie filling diluted with fruit juice or water makes a delicious sauce. Try any of the following favorites.

HOT LEMON SAUCE

1 pkg	lemon pudding and pie filling (4-serving size)	Make pudding as directed on package and use an additional ½ cup of water.
½ cup	water	

RICH LEMON SAUCE

3	egg yolks	In top of a double boiler, beat egg yolks; add sugar, lemon peel and lemon juice. Cook in double boiler over simmering water until thick. Cool. Whip cream and fold into sauce.
⅓ cup	sugar	
1 tbsp	lemon peel	
2 tbsp	lemon juice	
½ cup	whipping cream	

CHERRY SAUCE

¾ cup	cherry juice	Combine cherry juice, sugar, salt and cornstarch in saucepan. Cook over low heat for about 5 minutes, stirring constantly. Add remaining ingredients. Serve hot.
½ cup	sugar	
⅛ tsp	salt	
1½ tsp	cornstarch	
¼ cup	drained red, sour pitted cherries	
1 tbsp	butter	
1 tbsp	fresh lemon juice	

RUM SAUCE

1 cup	whipping cream
3	egg yolks
2 tbsp	sugar
⅓ cup	rum

Combine all ingredients in top of double boiler over simmering water. Cook and stir until slightly thickened.

CALIFORNIA WALNUT SAUCE

1 cup	light corn syrup
⅛ tsp	salt
¼ cup	water
¼ tsp	maple flavoring
1¼ cups	chopped walnuts

Bring syrup, salt, water and flavoring to a boil in a saucepan. Add walnuts, simmer slowly 15–20 minutes. Cool.

BUTTERY BLUEBERRY SAUCE

¼ cup	butter
⅔ cup	sugar
2 cups	fresh blueberries
¼ tsp	nutmeg
1 tbsp	lemon juice

Place all ingredients, except lemon juice, in saucepan and cook over low heat about 5 minutes. Stir in lemon juice. Serve warm over cake.

RUBY CRANBERRY SAUCE

½ cup	sugar
2 tbsp	cornstarch
2 cups	cranberry juice cocktail
1 tbsp	lemon juice

Place all ingredients in saucepan. Cook until thick and bubbly.

Whipped sauces may be served separately in a bowl, spread over a Bundt cake or heaped into the center of the cake. Fresh cream or whipped topping mix are equally suitable. For a festive touch, split the Bundt cake horizontally so it is in three layers; spread the flavored whipped topping between the layers.

BASIC WHIPPED TOPPING

2 cups   whipping cream
2-4 tbsp sugar
½ tsp   vanilla

In large bowl, whip cream until thickened; add sugar and vanilla and whip until dissolved.

CHOCOLATE: Add 2 tbsp cocoa to Basic.

CHOCOLATE #2: Add 2 tbsp chocolate flavored drink powder to whipped cream.

SPICE: Add ½ tsp cinnamon and ¼ tsp nutmeg to Basic.

COFFEE: Add ½ tsp instant coffee to Basic.

LEMON: Add 2 tbsp powdered lemonade concentrate to Basic and omit vanilla. Or, add ½ to 1 cup lemon pudding mix.

PRESERVE TOPPINGS: Add ½ cup fruit preserves to Basic and omit sugar and vanilla.

LIQUEUR FLAVORS: Add 1 to 2 tbsp rum, brandy, crème de cocoa, crème de menthe or any cordial of your choice to Basic. Omit vanilla.

APPLE: Fold whipped cream into 2 cups canned or cooked applesauce puree; add 1 tsp grated lemon peel and dash of cinnamon.

STRAWBERRY: Fold a 10-oz pkg frozen strawberries (thawed and drained) into whipped cream.

CRUSHED PEPPERMINT: Add ¼ cup crushed peppermint candy to white or chocolate whipped cream.

CRUSHED PEANUT BRITTLE: Add ¼ cup crushed peanut brittle to whipped cream.

OTHER IDEAS FOR YOUR
Bundt® pan

DISPLAY THEM PROUDLY!
If you have collected Bundt pans over the years and have a spare wall, hang your collection for all to see. Bundt pans not only bake beautiful cakes and breads, but each Bundt pan is truly a work of art!

CORRAL ODDS AND ENDS!
Tuck twine, ribbon, tags and scissors in a Bundt for a movable gift-wrapping station. Keep your sewing materials handy for quick repairs.

HAVE SOMETHING AWKWARD TO BAKE?
Use a Bundt pan to hold things like stuffed bell peppers to bake them safely upright.

USE THEM IN YOUR INDOOR AND OUTDOOR DÉCOR!
Bundt pans make great centerpieces when arranged with flowers and candles. Make a cute door hanger out of a "retired" Bundt pan with a coat of paint and a fancy ribbon. Plant a little succulent garden, herbs or petite flower varieties. Attach one to a garden stand for a birdbath.

MAKE AN ICE RING FOR A PUNCH BOWL!

Add berries and other fruits that flavor the punch as the ice melts. Use any of your beautiful Bundt pans or Bundlettes to create a unique and fun ice ring!

USE A BUNDT PAN FOR CLEANING CORN!

Place your Bundt pan open side up on a towel for stability. Stand the corn cob on the center and scrape off the kernels — the kernels are caught in the Bundt pan.

CREATE A WINTER WONDERLAND!

Freeze water in different shapes to create luminaries to line your walk in the winter. Just add candles to highlight the beautiful Bundt shapes.

FEED THE BIRDS!

Make a "cake" of seeds and nuts and a little peanut butter and hang it for your feathered friends.

INDEX

BREADS quick and yeast

SALADS